Honey...
Who Shrunk
Our
Money?

This edition published by
Global Professional Publishing Limited
The European Innovation Centre
Fitzroy House
11 Chenies Street
London WC1E 7EY

Printed by Yellow Digital

ISBN 978-0-85297-660-9

Curtis Arnold's
Honey...
Who Shrunk
Our
Money?

*To my wife, Judy,
without whose support
this book would not have been possible.*

Contents

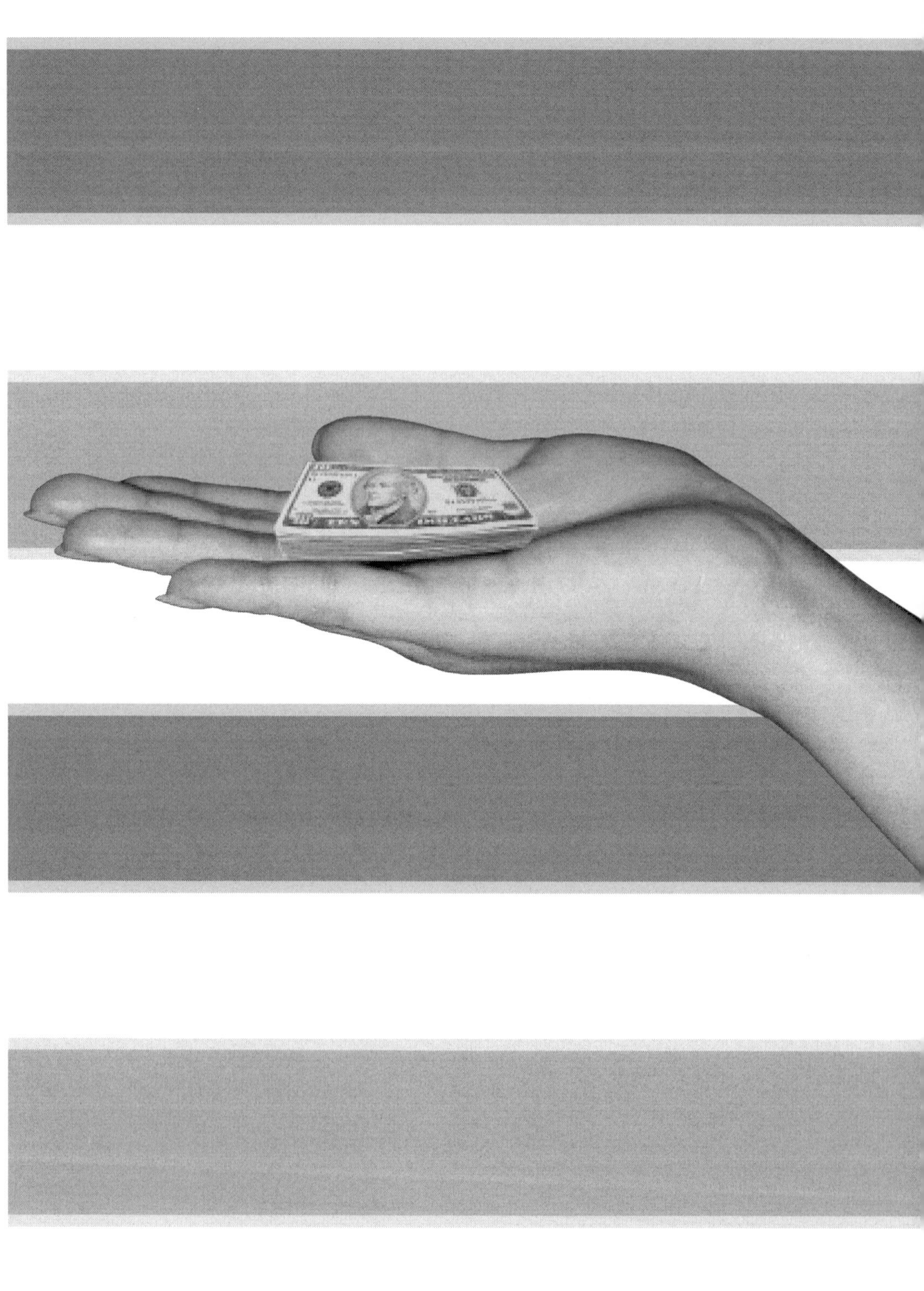

Preface

Back in 1978 I was fresh out of college, working in a small cubicle writing COBOL code. Today some of my friends are there still, hoping they make it to retirement before their projects are outsourced and their jobs are eliminated. I might still be there too had I not taken a gamble late one Tuesday afternoon. With sweaty palms and heart racing, I dialed my broker and made my first trade ever. "Buy me one June gold contract at the close," I ordered with as much authority as I could muster. That night I could hardly sleep, wondering where the price of gold would be the following day.

That day, lady luck was on my side. The price of gold was higher on Wednesday — and higher again on Thursday, and then again on Friday. That afternoon my broker called. "Son, it doesn't always work out like this. Maybe you'd better take your profit." On my broker's advice, I sold my position at the end of the week and pocketed nearly a half-year's wages. I had made my debut as a trader. The following Monday I tendered my resignation, and the markets have been my life and livelihood ever since.

Wiser with age, I have come to realize that luck and timing each play a far greater role in our fate than we care to admit. In hindsight, I have been lucky – lucky enough to get in early on some significant trends that allowed me to multiply my money. However, I have witnessed – and statistics bear it out – that most investors lose money. If not right away, then they lose it eventually, over time – victimized by insufficient knowledge, their own greed, or a bear market.

I am concerned that America's leaders have steered the country off course. In just several years, they have made a number of shortsighted policy decisions that have pushed the country closer to the day of financial reckoning. They borrowed recklessly and ran up a budget deficit with no plan to repay it. They covered up the truth about global warming, refusing to sign the Kyoto Treaty, which promotes the regulation of carbon dioxide emissions. They greatly expanded the military budget without just cause. They sat idly by while our manufacturing and high-paying jobs moved offshore. They created an enormous trade deficit, leaving us at the mercy of foreign nations. They looked the other way while industries such as Big Pharma and Big Oil raked in outlandish profits at the expense of average Americans. They ignored the future funding needs of Social Security and Medicare, content to pass the financial burden on to the next generation. Finally, they failed to act early enough to develop alternative energy sources, leaving us almost completely dependent on foreign oil.

These problems, which our government has created through bad policy, will affect all Americans. They will become a drag on the economy, markets, and your investments. Rising prices – especially for services such as health care and education – show no signs of slowing down. Meanwhile, wage growth and investment returns are not keeping pace. Thus, Americans who fail to make changes will face a declining standard of living.

However, these crises bring opportunity. You can protect your savings and even profit handsomely if you are willing to follow a new investment paradigm – one that seeks to profit from global trends that are already in place and will continue for the next decade. That is what I am doing. Remember, I am a trader first (a hedge fund manager) and a writer second. The very advice I give in this book I implement in my own investing. You *can* turn America's woes into your good fortune if you start now and stay the course. Good luck and let me know how you do!

~ Curtis Arnold

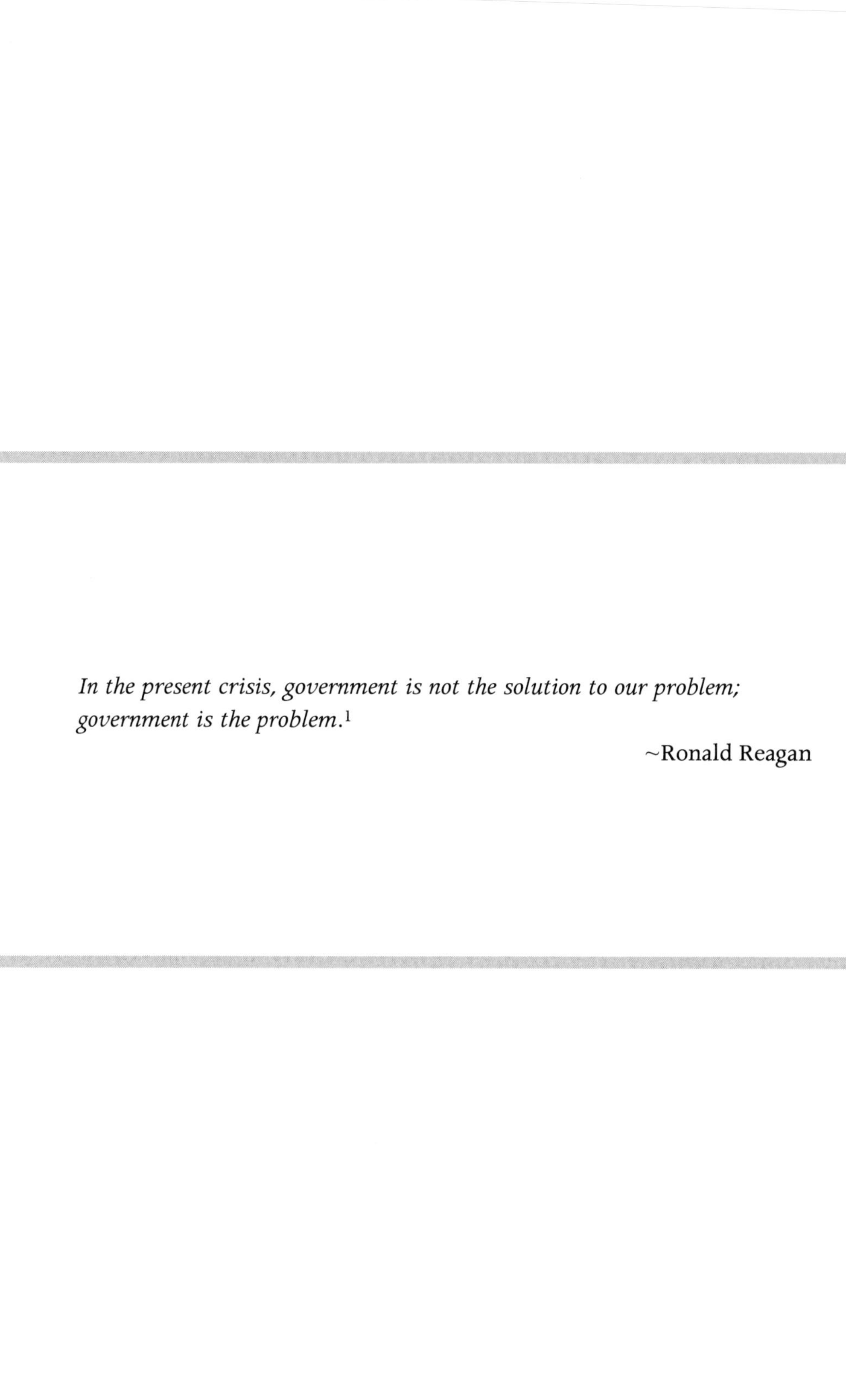

In the present crisis, government is not the solution to our problem; government is the problem.[1]

~Ronald Reagan

America's Woes

Games Governments Play

The best way to destroy the capitalist system is to debauch the currency. By a continuing process of inflation, governments can confiscate, secretly and unobserved, an important part of the wealth of their citizens.[1]

~ John Maynard Keynes

In America today, millions of people who once led comfortable middle-class lives now find themselves straining against an inflationary headwind. Trapped by stagnant wages on the one hand and a rising cost of living on the other, they worry that they will not have the money they will need to pay their bills in the future. Are their concerns justified? Absolutely.

In fact, despite what the government would like you to believe, inflation is already at work like a silent thief, eroding the hard-earned savings of Americans and making a sham of the paltry cost-of-living wage increases doled out by corporate America. However, the inflation we have seen recently (underreported by the government) pales in comparison to what is just around the corner. The United States government, already hopelessly in debt, will soon require enormous sums of money to prevent the economy from backsliding into a severe recession. The money required to pay our growing debts, whether it comes via foreign borrowing by the Treasury Department or via credit supplied by the Federal Reserve, will guarantee a higher cost of living.

While rising prices will pose severe financial consequences for most people, this book will show you how to safeguard your savings and investments and profit from the coming inflation. First, however, let's examine the prospects for Americans to get ahead in the workplace.

The Glass Ceiling on Wages

The truth is that many Americans could face a financial future even bleaker than they expect. American workers have cause for worry. Outsourcing and offshoring jeopardize an increasing number of industries. What began as a trickle will soon become a flood as a growing number of productive enterprises (and high-paying jobs) move offshore. With recent strides in global communication, including the World Wide Web, any task that can be digitized can be performed more cheaply and often more efficiently overseas.

Globalization may one day jeopardize traditionally secure careers. For example, during the 1970s, future demand for computer professionals seemed assured. No one could have anticipated that within a few decades American IT professionals would have to compete with programmers from India in the global marketplace. Now, Andy Grove of Intel warns that the U.S. software industry could become an endangered species.[2] American engineers must also compete with Indian engineers who work for one-fourth the wage of their American counterparts. Even financial services are at risk; a Deloitte research study, surveying one hundred of the country's largest financial service firms, predicted that two million jobs would move offshore between 2005 and 2010.[3]

If your future income is uncertain, you have an even greater incentive to learn how to maximize your investment returns. Even if your job is secure, you may sense that your money does not go as far as it did just a few years ago. Is it true? Is your money shrinking? The answer is yes. It is, it has been for some time, and it will get even worse. Before learning why, however, we need to clear up a major misconception about inflation. In fact, it is time we exposed one of the government's most far-reaching falsehoods.

The Big CPI Lie

Mark Twain said, "There are three kinds of lies: Lies, damned lies and statistics." The Consumer Price Index (CPI), which purportedly measures the rate of inflation, is a great illustration of Twain's observation. This one magical number supposedly can tell us how much more or less it is costing us to live. The financial media receive the number from the Bureau of Labor Statistics each month and report it to the public, much like this: "The Consumer Price Index dropped by three-tenths of a percent last month, bringing the annual inflation rate down to $3\frac{1}{2}$ percent." End of story. We now know everything we need to know about inflation. Inflation is low, so what's the big deal?

It would not be a big deal if it were true, but if it is true, why does it feel like nearly everything you do costs more and some things cost a lot more? We all know that it costs more to drive our cars, insure our houses, pay our property taxes, and go out for an evening's entertainment. Is the government living in inflation denial or purposely lying to us? Why would they lie to us? What would they have to gain? Let's see.

Assume that the government reports that the Consumer Price Index is increasing at 4 percent per year. How could that affect you? First, many employers base their annual wage increases on the CPI. Your employer might give you an annual cost of living increase of 4 percent to match the CPI. However, what if the CPI failed to reflect the true rate of inflation? What if the true rate of inflation was not 4 percent, but 8 percent? You would find yourself falling behind. If this discrepancy continued for more than a year, your purchasing power would diminish at an increasing rate each year. The following example will illustrate how.

Assume that your gross pay is $1,000 per week. If your employer matches your wage increase to the reported CPI, you would make an extra $40 per week. However, after the taxman visits, your net raise might be closer to $30 per week. Given that the true rate of inflation is 8 percent, it would cost you an additional $50 per week to live ($80 − $30). Because of the effect of compounding, however, each year the gap between your take-home pay and your cost of living would widen. For many Americans, this gap has led to excessive credit card borrowing and the use of home equity loans to keep up.

Your savings are shrinking also. Because of the correlation between interest rates and the CPI, a low CPI translates into a low return on your savings. Therefore, if the reported CPI is lower than the true rate of inflation, the difference between the two is your loss. To illustrate, assume that you have invested $10,000 that returns 4 percent per year in interest. If the true inflation rate was actually 8 percent, the purchasing power of your savings would also decline at a frightening pace. In the example in table 1.1, I have assumed that your tax rate is 26 percent and have rounded all numbers to the nearest dollar.

Now we are ready to answer the question that I proposed earlier. What would the government have to gain by reporting artificially low Consumer Price Index numbers? A bit of thought reveals how much they would have to lose if they did not.

- Large unions would go on strike, demanding higher wages to keep up with the cost of living.
- Social Security benefits (indexed to wage increases) would rise, costing the government more money.
- Interest rates would increase accordingly, costing the government hundreds of billions of dollars more each year in interest on the national debt.

As you can see, the government has a lot to gain by reporting artificially low CPI numbers and a lot to lose by reporting high ones. But the question remains, do they? I can't answer that, but I will say that the CPI does not adequately measure the cost of living. Let me explain.

The Consumer Price Index measures the prices of a market basket of 211 goods and services that consumers normally buy. In theory, the CPI

Table 1.1 Money (Savings) Shrinking

Year	Starting Value of Savings	Gross Interest	After Tax Interest	Ending Value of Savings	Cost of Living	Difference Lost	Value of $1 of savings (rounded to nearest penny)
1	$1000.00	$40.00	$29.60	$1029.60	$1080.00	$50.40	95¢
2	$1029.60	$41.18	$30.48	$1060.08	$1166.40	$106.32	88¢
3	$1060.08	$42.40	$31.38	$1091.46	$1259.71	$168.25	87¢
4	$1091.46	$43.66	$32.31	$1123.77	$1360.49	$236.72	83¢
5	$1123.77	$44.95	$33.26	$1157.03	$1469.33	$312.30	79¢

is supposed to act as a proxy for consumers' cost of living. However, I believe that it does a poor job. Here are four reasons why:

1. The market basket of 211 goods and services is underweighted on services.
2. The market basket is out of date.
3. The CPI does not account for the true cost of home ownership.
4. The CPI cannot account for the variability in individual spending patterns.

The first reason that the CPI does a poor job is because the market basket is underweighted on services, and that is where we tend to spend most of our money. A few of the services not included in the market basket are movie tickets, greens fees, lift tickets, tickets to a ball game, and concert tickets. In fact, most of the things that you "do" — as opposed to things that you "buy" — do not show up in the CPI.

The second reason that the CPI does a poor job is because the market basket is out of date; the Bureau of Labor Statistics updates the basket only every ten years. Therefore, the CPI does not know much about my spending habits. It does not know that everyone in my family has a cell phone and that we pay extra for DSL service for our computers. Neither does it take into consideration that we subscribe to both XM radio and TIVO. I won't belabor the point, which is quite simply that the CPI fails the relevancy test in my life and probably yours too. It may have practically nothing to do with your real cost of living.

The third reason that the CPI does a poor job is because the CPI does not account for the true cost of home ownership. In short, the government assumes that we are all renting our dwellings. Given that 85 percent of Americans own their own homes, how reasonable is that? Moreover, everyone knows that the price to rent a house relative to the price of buying a house is at an all-time low. Here's an example of how that practice skews the numbers: I own a $500,000 condominium that I rent out for $1,500 a month. If you wanted to buy the condominium, your total payments including taxes and maintenance would run close to $3,000 a month. However, if you bought my condominium, the Bureau of Labor Statistics would record $1,500 rather than $3,000 because that is the current costs of rentals in that complex. By not including the real costs of home ownership, which includes property taxes and homeowner's insurance, the government can more easily report artificially low CPI numbers.

The fourth reason that the CPI does a poor job is because it cannot account for the variability in our individual spending patterns. For example, imagine how differently inflation might affect the following stereotypical people who live on Elm Street in a small town in suburban America. Katy Smith, 26, is an unmarried attorney residing at 101 Elm Street. She may be less at risk than Bill and Rita Jones who live across the street at 102 Elm Street. The Jones's cost of living will certainly get a jolt when they send their two daughters to private colleges in the fall. (College tuition, which has been rising at double-digit rates, is not included in the CPI.) Fred and Marie Emerson, retirees who live next door to Katy at 103 Elm Street, are struggling as well. In poor health, they spend a significant portion of their income on prescription medicines, which have been rising at twice the rate of inflation for years.

In summary, inflation is higher than you think and it is eroding your purchasing power. The uncertainty of future employment, resulting from the trends of outsourcing and offshoring, further threaten your ability to keep up with the rising cost of living. Moreover, if I am right, even greater inflation lies ahead. By taking the time to read this book in its entirety and then implementing the strategies in part 2, you will be able to protect yourself from being mugged by inflation and quite possibly profit handsomely because of it.

A Simple 4-Step Plan

This book will give you a 4-step plan that will allow you to create a fortune from the coming inflation. Once you learn all four steps, you will be in a position to take advantage of the coming inflation. Moreover, you will see that you have a once in a lifetime opportunity to create wealth — the kind that would normally require a lifetime of saving and investing — in just a few short years. Here are the four steps to the plan.

Step 1

Step 1 requires learning how inflation works and understanding the seven geopolitical trends that will contribute to a rising tide of inflation. Without that knowledge, you will not succeed. That is because secular market trends — the kind that last for years and can make you a fortune — are not one-way streets. There will be countertrends against your positions that shake your confidence. Without an unfailing conviction that you are right, you will surely fail.

The Federal Reserve, which will take action to contain the rising tide of inflation, will cause the countertrends. At other times, they will take action to prevent a recession and those actions will benefit your positions. An example of that occurred after the stock market crash in 2000, when the Fed immediately reduced short-term interest rates, specifically to prevent a recession.

After the economy regained its momentum and the real estate market reached bubble proportions, the Fed became more worried about inflation than recession so they attempted to slow the rate of inflation by increasing interest rates. Higher interest rates act to slow the rate of inflation, but have an unwanted side effect of slowing the economy. During an interest rate tightening cycle, at some point the Fed must stop raising interest rates or risk a recession. If the economy slows too much, the Fed has no choice but to reduce interest rates again, which leads to more inflation. Regardless of what phase the interest cycle is in at the time you read this book, know that the perfect financial storm is inevitable regardless of interest rate policy.

The perfect financial storm — a culmination of seven geopolitical trends — virtually guarantees inflation. Like an incoming tide, inflation will be a secular trend – that is, one that will last for years to come. The Federal Reserve's attempts to control the economy by manipulating interest rates will not be sufficient to override the onslaught of inflation.

Step 2

Step 2 requires learning how to use easy money. Easy money means money that is readily available at low rates of interest. Unless you already have savings, the ability to borrow money is critical to your success. In no time in history has it been easier to borrow money, so lack of money should not be an excuse. Certainly, millions of Americans have discovered that they can easily borrow money and have used home equity lines to access this easy money. Unfortunately, most have spent the money instead of investing it.

Did you ever wonder why banking is one of the most profitable businesses in the world? It is because banks are first in line when money roles off the printing presses. The federal government creates the money that allows our society to exist. Banks are the intermediary between the government's printing presses and the public. Money is like any other product. Banks get it wholesale and lend it out — invest their money — at retail. To build your fortune, you will need to start thinking like a bank.

Does that mean that you will lend out your money once you borrow it? No. Like banks, you will seek to make a profit on your investments, but you will not be loaning money because loaning money is not a good business during times of inflation. You will make other types of investments — specifically, the kind that will benefit from inflation.

Step 3

Step 3 requires that you learn how to spot investments that will benefit from inflation. This book will show you several broad asset classes that will benefit from inflation, and offer you dozens of specific investments for your consideration.

Step 4

Step 4 requires that you learn how to use various investment vehicles to take advantage of those investment opportunities. Why is it important to understand how to use different kinds of investment vehicles? Think of investment vehicles as modes of transportation that will take you to your destination. For example, imagine that you would like to go somewhere. It could be a neighbor's house, the grocery store, or a relative's house in another state. The distance to your destination might be the determining factor in your choice of transportation – your vehicle. You may choose to ride your bike to the neighbors, drive your car to the store, and take a plane to visit your relative. To arrive successfully at those destinations would require you to know how to ride a bike, drive a car, and purchase an airline ticket.

Similarly, when investing in an asset or company that will benefit from inflation, you may wish to use an ETF (exchange-traded fund), a stock, an option, or a futures contract. Don't worry if you have never made these types of investments before or even if you are not certain what they are. There are many ways that even a novice investor can take advantage of inflation. For now, you simply need to be aware of the four steps in the plan.

You are now ready to begin with the first part of step 1, which is to learn how inflation works. Inflation is nothing new. Nation after nation has crumbled because of mismanagement of the money supply by their government. It will continue to happen as long as governments issue fiat currencies. By learning a little about past inflations and their consequences, you will better understand our current state of affairs brought about by shortsighted politicians who inevitably choose to spend more than they should at the expense of future generations.

The First Inflation

In the ancient world, there were no ATMs, no credit cards, no checks, and no paper currency. Money exchanged hands by way of coins. Coins were made of gold, silver, and bronze. Like today, gold coins were the most valuable, then silver coins, and, finally, bronze coins.

The Roman Empire's success depended upon wealth acquired by conquering neighboring lands. Thus, as the Romans conquered more lands, the empire grew ever wealthier. Once Romans ran out of territory to conquer, the empire stopped expanding and began to run short of money. Rome struggled to pay its soldiers stationed at far-flung outposts, maintain its infrastructure, and support its social programs (200,000 people existed on welfare in the city of Rome).

In ancient times, governments debased their currency by adding fillers of base metals to their coins. They pulled this trick whenever their own currency — coins made of gold, silver, or bronze — was in short supply. By adding the fillers, they could make far more coins, thus increasing the money supply.

Therefore, while it is true that Rome eventually fell to barbarian invasions in the fifth century, the underlying cause of the fall of this great empire was inflation caused by fiscal mismanagement. Quite simply, they spent more than they made. To stay in power, emperors courted favor with the masses by creating a welfare state and maintaining large armies dispersed over far-flung lands. Consider the parallels to America today.

Too Much of a Good Thing

In the 1500s, Spain was the greatest and richest empire in the world. It controlled most of what is now Italy, the Netherlands, the Philippines, the West Indies, Central America, and most of South America. The 1500s were considered the golden age in Spain in both literature and painting. What caused this empire to flourish was the large amount of precious metals (wealth) brought into the country from other nations. The largest part of this wealth was in the form of silver, which came from mines in Mexico and Peru.

At the time, Spain believed that precious metals were the true form of wealth and that accumulating precious metals should be the number one priority of the state. To that end, they engaged in mining, piracy, and conquest. The wealth enriched Spain's royalty and the church. It outfitted the army and navy, and it allowed for the import of exotic goods from the East.

As more silver came into the country, prices began to rise. Wage earners grumbled, as did exporters who found it difficult to sell in foreign markets. But no one really understood that the source of the inflation came from the abundance of silver, which was thought to be wealth. More units of the precious metal were required to buy the same amount of wheat or a quantity of labor, and so the prices of both increased. The higher price of wheat — traded internationally — affected both neighboring France and, to a lesser degree, England. Thus, Spain unknowingly exported its inflation to its neighbors.

Spain's leaders' biggest mistake was their assumption that precious metals alone would make Spain a powerful country. Flush with wealth, they failed to invest in basic industry and productive enterprises. Instead, Spain spent the vast majority of the wealth on its military, engaged throughout the world. They spent the rest on ornamentation, shrines, and other excesses of royalty. By 1600, the well had run dry due to a diminished flow of silver from American mines. Like Rome, revenues no longer kept pace with the fixed expenses of the government, prompting a long decline of this once great empire.

This historical example provides a great lesson. When money comes from outside a country's borders, it causes inflation unless channeled into means of production — the only true wealth. That is why China wisely invests part of the revenues they receive from exports in capital stock (factories) and sends the rest back to America. (You will learn exactly how they do that in a later chapter.)

The Greenback Dollar

The outbreak of the Civil War required each side to raise money quickly to finance their military efforts. Both sides had only three alternatives: raise money through taxes, borrow money, or print money. Each side used a combination of all three, but, in the end, both sides financed the majority of the cost of the war by printing money. The North issued a new currency called "Greenbacks" because of the color of the ink used in printing. It was a fiat currency from the beginning because it was not convertible to gold. A currency is called "fiat" when it has no value other than the promise made by the government that issued it. Paper, of course, has no value in and of itself. When a currency is not linked to a commodity that has value, such as gold, it can depreciate rapidly. During the course of the Civil War, prices approximately doubled in the North because of the depreciation of the Greenback.

The Confederates did not fare well with their financing efforts either. Thus, they quickly resorted to printing Confederate notes. These began to depreciate even quicker than the Union's Greenback dollars, and, as the war wore on, the increased money in circulation began to chase a diminishing quantity of goods. By the end of the war, prices had increased some twenty-eight-fold.

Two Beers, Please

The German inflation of 1922-1923 was the granddaddy of inflations. In Germany, the government in power turned on the printing presses full throttle. Why? After Germany lost World War I, the country found itself with huge financial debts that it could not pay; their leaders believed they had no other choice but to print money in order to meet the country's obligations. The money printing soon led to an inflationary spiral that they were unable to stop.

At the height of the inflation, supposedly people stood in lines with wheelbarrows of money to buy a loaf of bread. Other manifestations of Germany's inflation are equally incredible. For example, at one point, factories paid workers twice a day. If workers did not spend their money right away, it would lose considerable value. After their shifts ended, workers ordered two beers at once, fearing the price of the second beer might be higher if they waited until they finished the first. There was a bright side: if someone bought a bottle of wine, he was often able to sell the empty bottle for more the next day than he had paid for the full bottle.

The German inflation wiped out the value of all the savings of the middle class. Economic chaos ensued and along with it political chaos and uncertainty. The German people were thus receptive to new ideas. Not long after that, Hitler emerged on the scene. When you think that

Hitler might never have come to power if inflation had not devastated the middle class, you cannot help but worry about the ultimate consequences of inflation in this or any country.

Hey Buddy, Can You Spare a Dime?

In 1922, the federal government gave the Reserve Banks the authority to regulate credit conditions by buying and selling government securities. In 1924, they used that authority to stimulate the economy. Granted, the Reserve Banks overdid it somewhat. An economic boom transpired and it soon got out of hand. Speculation ran rampant, first in the Florida land boom and later in the overheated stock market. Additionally, for the first time in history, one could buy stocks on margin, a policy that encouraged even further speculation.

In October 1928, Benjamin Strong, the much-heralded head of the Federal Reserve, passed away, leaving the institution divided and leaderless. As a result, the Fed failed to tighten credit while they still had the chance. As we know, all speculative frenzies end. This one ended because excessive credit caused businesses to expand too rapidly. Excess capacity then caused corporate profits to decline. Excessive credit creation causes booms that eventually bust when investors realize that the assets (stocks or real estate) do not produce a commensurate return on investment. Eventually, the public realized that the prices of stocks were not justified by earnings and they began to sell. The market crashed on October 29, 1929, which also marked the beginning of the Great Depression.

Having failed to tighten credit when they should have, the Fed did just the opposite after the crash occurred. Between 1929 and 1933, the Fed cut the money supply by one-third. In so doing, they converted a serious but normal slowdown into a catastrophic recession. Because of this, there is near universal agreement among scholars that serious incompetence at the Federal Reserve aggravated the Great Depression.

Inflation in the Twentieth Century

When we reflect on our own personal history and that of our parents, we often refer to an age by citing a decade — for example, the band played fifties music or she was a child of the sixties. The name of a decade alone conjures up specific images, which define a way of life for the period. By examining inflation from this social context, we can appreciate how inflation affects our lives.

During the first decade of the 1900s, inflation averaged 15 percent because our government printed money to finance World War I. During the 1920s, inflation averaged zero percent. Are you surprised? You shouldn't be. Business was good, which is usually the case when inflation is low. However, not unlike today, while we did not experience consumer inflation in the 1920s, we did experience asset bubbles in the stock market and selected real estate markets because of easy credit. In the 1930s, the average inflation rate was negative $1\frac{1}{2}$ percent. The deflation of the decade led to high unemployment and general misery. The 1940s average inflation rate was negative 1 percent. For the first half of the decade America struggled with a weak economy. In the second half of the decade, the economy began a recovery that would last for two decades.

The 1950s saw inflation average 1 percent. It was an era of rising optimism and good business conditions. The stock market nearly doubled from 1953 to 1955. Just as the 1920s saw the radio as a sign of strong technological progress, which boosted public optimism, the television came into widespread use in the 1950s, creating the same effect. Many couples had babies and moved from small apartments to new three-bedroom homes.

In 1960, John Kennedy became president. He expanded confidence in the country with his economic stimulus programs and ambitious space programs. The 1960s saw inflation rise to an average of 5 percent. After the Kennedy assassination, the mood of the country changed. Eventually, the good feelings that had lasted throughout the 1950s and into the early 1960s gave way to resentment and mistrust because of the Vietnam War.

By the 1970s, inflation averaged 11 percent. Excessive money printing to finance the war and Johnson's Great Society programs set the stage for inflation. High energy prices (oil reached the equivalent of $100 a barrel in today's dollars) dealt the final blow, sending the economy into stagflation. (Stagflation occurs when prices and unemployment are rising but there is little growth in consumer demand and business activity.) By the 1980s, the Fed's austerity, under the leadership of Paul Volker, brought the average inflation rate for the decade down to 5 percent and launched what would become the greatest stock market boom in our lifetimes. Inflation in the 1990s averaged only 2 percent, allowing business confidence to build and the stock market boom to continue.

The record clearly reinforces the point that the economy thrives when inflation is low and suffers when inflation is high. Furthermore, it shows us that deflation is most undesirable as it goes hand in hand with depression and high unemployment. Clearly, history has proven it is necessary to walk a fine line with inflation: It must be kept low (2 percent to 5 percent has proven ideal), but it cannot be allowed to go negative, which by definition would then be deflation.

We must be aware that the overall inflation rate has little effect on asset bubbles and busts. During the 1920s, although inflation was low, the credit-induced stock market bubble eventually wiped out the savings of millions of Americans when it burst. Fortunately, the Fed learned from its past mistakes and acted quickly to reduce rates after the NASDAQ crash, thus saving the country from the very real threat of another depression. However, years later, many people are still wondering why the NASDAQ crash occurred. Was inflation a factor?

Irrational Exuberance

The term *irrational exuberance* gained national attention in 1997 when Alan Greenspan used it to characterize the stock market boom. Months later, to the confusion of everyone, he changed his tune, claiming that we were in a "new era."

At what point does a boom become a bubble? I suppose every bubble begins as a boom and at some point along the way turns into a bubble. The great bull market in stocks from 1982 to 2000 would fit that description. The majority of the bull market was justified by strong fundamentals. Inflation was 4 percent at the beginning of the bull market and later dropped to 3, and finally 2 percent. Additionally, the tax climate was excellent. In 1997, Congress cut the top capital gains rate from 28 percent to 20 percent. Talk of further cuts lent credence to holding stocks until lower tax rates would take effect.

A constant influx of money from the mutual fund industry acted as a growth hormone to the market throughout the 1990s. During the bull market, the number of mutual funds increased ten-fold, while the number of people owning mutual funds grew from 6.2 million in 1982 to 119.8 million in 1998.[4] The main source of mutual fund growth was a phenomenal increase in the number of 401(k)s. Prior to 1981, most employees owned defined-benefit plans, which paid a fixed pension to them upon retirement. In 1981, 401(k) plans were created that allowed employees to contribute tax-deferred amounts from their paychecks, which employers often matched. More importantly, the plans allowed employees to invest their contributions in a wide selection of mutual funds.

While these were all powerful drivers of the bull market, when a boom turns into a bubble, common sense goes out the window. By 1997, justifying the fundamentals became increasingly difficult. By that time, the price-to-earnings ratio on stocks had surpassed its former record high set in September 1929, just weeks before the Great Crash. That meant that investors were overpaying for stocks, but no one on Wall Street was about to tell them.

In 1999, just prior to the crash, only 1 percent of analysts' recommendations were sells.[5] There are two reasons analysts rarely issue sell recommendations. The first is that the companies will exclude them from any further interviews or access to their key executives when they are preparing earning forecasts. The second is that often their own brokerage firms have underwriting deals with those same companies. In 1999, well-known interest rate analyst James Grant wrote, "Honesty was never a profit center on Wall Street, but the brokers used to keep up appearances. Now they have stopped pretending. More than ever, securities research is a branch of sales. Investor, beware."[6]

When the stock market bubble burst in 2000, the reasons were no different from any other bubble. Stocks were wildly overvalued; businesses had expanded too quickly and had taken on too much debt; and, the companies were saturated with technology. First, Internet stocks fell, then the rest of the tech market, and finally the whole market itself.

The country narrowly avoided a steep recession only because the Fed ratcheted interest rates down quickly. The low interest rates offered by banks for mortgage financing ignited the real estate boom, which eventually took on the same psychological characteristics that fueled the stock market just a few years earlier. We will study the real estate market in some depth in chapter 11. Next, however, you are going to learn about the underlying problem in the economy that lies at the root of future inflation.

The Crux of the Problem

Despite a façade of prosperity, the American economy is in serious trouble. The underlying problem is that we are no longer a productive nation. A productive nation produces more than it consumes and sells the difference by way of exports. Those businesses that produce and export their products reinvest the profits in their businesses. Thus, the country develops greater wealth over time. China is an example of a country that grows richer and stronger each year because it is able to export more than it imports.

In America, the process that allows a country to develop wealth has broken down. Each year our country produces less. Because it continues to consume more than it makes, it must import a portion of what it needs from other countries. Moreover, in order to stay competitive in a global marketplace, American businesses are building manufacturing plants overseas where labor is cheaper. Over time, the country grows weaker because its means of production decrease. Capital stock is another term for means of production, or factories, and I will use the terms interchangeably.

America was able to create wealth throughout the 1800s and 1900s because of two reasons. First, it was rich in natural resources, like oil. Until fairly recently, America had a surplus of oil and exported more than it produced. Now, it must import most of the oil it consumes. The second reason that America was able to create wealth is that our ancestors built buildings, machines, and factories, which they bequeathed to the younger generation. As long as this process continued, each generation became wealthier than the previous one.

Savings are a critical component to the investment process that allows a country to build its means of production. Savings are the fuel that feeds the engine of investment, which creates the means of production. Here is how it works: when Americans save part of their income, those savings go into banks, and the banks then lend that money to businesses. Businesses use the money to create new factories — means of production.

Our savings rate has dropped to near zero. Some studies show that the savings rate is negative, meaning that the average American spends more than he makes. This breakdown of savings and investment is a recipe for economic disaster. The United States finds itself in that situation today, though few acknowledge the severity of the problem. Either our politicians do not appreciate the impending crisis or they are more attuned to their own agendas.

The current generation is consuming the country's capital rather than building it. By spending more than we produce and sending that money overseas, we transfer about 1 percent of our wealth to foreigners each year. As a result, America's current generation will leave less capital stock to its heirs. Because of misguided American policy, the next generation will be the first in our country's history to have less than their parents.

A Temporary Fix with Long-Term Consequences

After the stock market crash in 2000, the Federal Reserve was quick to stimulate the economy by reducing short-term interest rates from 6 percent down to 1 percent in a series of aggressive rate cuts. Had they not, the country would have slipped into a much deeper recession. While the economy faltered for a few quarters, the easy money eventually worked its magic. Homeowners borrowed money using home equity lines and spent the money either remodeling their homes or paying off balances on high interest rate credit cards.

Subsequent to the stock market crash, credit creation totaled over six trillion dollars during a three-year period. Where did all the money go?

A significant portion went into housing. Lower interest rates allowed consumers to qualify for much higher mortgages and afford more expensive homes.

The government calls a rise in stock prices or housing prices a "wealth effect." However, a rise in the value of stocks or real estate is not true wealth. For example, if the market value of your house increases by $100,000, the house did not suddenly become better. Moreover, you are no better off by selling your house if the next house you buy also costs $100,000 more.

Instead of wealth creation, what we are currently experiencing is nothing more than asset inflation, which has taken the form of a real estate bubble in some parts of the country. Asset bubbles make people feel wealthier and so they spend more, whether they can afford to or not. The government knows that and knows that a real estate asset bubble is even more potent than a stock market bubble because more people own real estate. Therefore, the government intentionally created the bubble not only by lowering interest rates but also by creating quasi-governmental agencies such as Fannie Mae and Freddie Mac that would buy the mortgages banks created.

Did you ever wonder why banks are so eager to lend you money on your house? It is because they no longer have any risk. They sell their loans as soon as they make them to agencies like Fannie Mae. Fannie Mae buys the loans at a discount and uses low-interest-rate money provided by the government to make the purchases. Fannie Mae then bundles the loans and sells the packages to pension funds, insurance companies, and foreign investors. Therefore, asset inflation is a house of cards built on debt that is passed from one investor to another like a hot potato.

Counting on Consumers

When the economy was healthy, the consumer accounted for about two-thirds of gross domestic product (GDP), while business spending and investment accounted for the remaining third. Now, consumer spending accounts for nearly 90 percent of GDP. If Americans cut back on their spending even a little, the economy will slip quickly into a recession.

How frightening is it to think that our economy is dependent on consumers whose wages are not increasing significantly and who are up to their eyeballs in debt? Despite what the government calls wealth creation, the average homeowner has less equity in his house now than he did before the real estate boom. Furthermore, his savings are lower and his debts are higher. If the consumer is truly tapped out, where will the money come from to keep the economy rolling? The answer to that question is that the Federal Reserve will have no choice but to infuse the system with money, which will lead to more inflation.

What will it take to keep the economy rolling? More than anyone anticipates. We'll learn why in the next chapter. The country is facing a number of crises that will cause government expenditures to rise far in excess of what people expect. Learning the truth about these ticking time bombs, while unsettling, should give you the resolve needed to harness the coming inflation (the consequence of the government's insatiable need for money) to protect your assets and build a fortune. All it takes is a willingness to learn and the courage to apply what you learn.

2

Seven Ticking Time Bombs

*The budget should be balanced; the treasury should be refilled;
the public debt should be reduced; and the arrogance of public
officials should be controlled.*

~ Cicero 106 — 43 B.C.

Successful investors always make money by anticipating the future, not reacting to it. Moreover, they understand how monetary and fiscal policy works to produce market trends. Monetary policy is about money supply and interest rates, which are the responsibility of the Federal Reserve. Fiscal policy is about taxes and spending, which are the responsibility of Congress and the Administration. The inflation of the 1970s was a direct result of prior budget deficits (fiscal policy) and easy money (monetary policy). Astute investors, who were able to anticipate the inflation those policies would cause, made fortunes.

After the 1970s inflation, however, a period of disinflation followed. To profit, you would have needed the foresight that restrictive Federal Reserve policies would ultimately lead to disinflation. With that understanding, you could have liquidated inflation-based investments at a handsome profit and reallocated your portfolio to profit from disinflation.

Because of changing monetary and fiscal policies, the economy will always be in one of the following five states:

Deflation, disinflation, stable inflation, rising inflation, and hyperinflation.

Deflation occurs when the inflation rate is negative. Disinflation occurs when inflation is still above zero but is declining. Stable inflation means that the general price level is neither rising nor declining. Rising inflation means that the rate of inflation is trending higher, and hyperinflation indicates that the rate of price increases have spiraled out of control. You can make money — a lot of money — by understanding how monetary and fiscal policies work to produce the next state and investing accordingly. If you skipped your economics class, don't worry; it's not that hard.

Our current economic state is always the cumulative result of monetary and fiscal policies — that is, decisions made by numerous administrations and Federal Reserve boards — of the past several decades. Examining those policies and their consequences in the economy will convince you how important it is to monitor both fiscal and monetary policy. Additionally, you will see how cumulative policies have brought us to the brink of economic disaster.

Ticking Time Bomb #1 ~ The Budget Deficit

During most of America's history, our politicians were fiscally responsible. If the government needed money, it would raise taxes, and it only permitted deficits during times of war. Under John F. Kennedy's administration, the United States experienced a booming economy and low inflation. Economically, it was our country's finest hour. Then, on November 22, 1963, the world changed. I will begin the story there because that was the genesis of modern-day inflation.

The Presidential Hall of Shame

To assess the damage done to future generations, I will issue each of our presidents since Kennedy a grade based on his ability to control the federal budget. Here's the grading scale: poor *, fair **, good ***, and excellent ****.

- Lyndon Johnson *
- Richard Nixon **
- Gerald Ford *
- Jimmy Carter *
- Ronald Reagan *
- George Bush Sr. *
- Bill Clinton ****
- George W. Bush *

*Lyndon Johnson *

The assassination of President Kennedy ushered in the Johnson administration, and American fiscal policy quickly veered off course. Lyndon Johnson spent money that the country simply did not have. His Great Society programs — while they did much to promote noble social causes — were costly. Prior to Johnson's administration, our only entitlement program was Social Security. He added Medicare, Medicaid, and several other smaller entitlement programs. With all these entitlement programs, the benefits are automatic and require no subsequent review or appropriation. Only an act of Congress could curtail them. Of course, any attempts at cutbacks would be politically unfeasible.

In addition to expensive social programs, Johnson borrowed heavily to finance the Vietnam War. Johnson ran budget deficits five years in a row. Those deficits then set the stage for the inflation that was to follow in the 1970s. Moreover, Johnson's policies that condoned deficit spending set a bad precedent for future administrations.

*Richard Nixon **

Richard Nixon inherited the fiscal mess that Johnson had created. To his credit, he did recognize the errors that Johnson had made and attempted to correct them. He immediately reduced military spending and established caps on some of the entitlement programs. During 1969, his first year in office, the country ran a small budget surplus. Over his entire six years in office, however, the national debt (the cumulative result of yearly budget deficits) grew by $67 billion, exceeding the nearly $45 billion that Johnson had added. Like Johnson, Nixon made a fiscal mistake that would cost future administrations billions. In 1972, he indexed Social Security benefits to the rate of inflation, thus practically guaranteeing that costs for this entitlement program would rise every year.

Gerald Ford ✱

Gerald Ford became president in 1974 after Nixon resigned in disgrace. His term was the shortest of all modern presidents — a scant two years. The country was already in recession and inflation was running high. The combination of the two, called stagflation, is one of the most difficult economic conditions to treat. As had been common political practice during times of recession, Ford decided to stimulate the economy. His first act was a tax rebate in 1974, which was followed by a tax cut in 1975. He hoped that by putting more money in consumers' hands, the public would spend their way out of recession. The effect of the extra money in the economy, however, simply acted to push inflation even higher. In his two short years in office, Ford contributed nearly $127 billion to the national debt – more than Johnson and Nixon managed in eleven years.

Jimmy Carter ✱

Jimmy Carter did very little to help the economy. While he might have cut back entitlement programs or defense spending, he chose to do neither. Instead, he continued to run the country on deficit spending. Stagflation persisted. Interest rates outpaced inflation, the prime reaching an unprecedented 21 percent in 1980.

With inflation running high, the indexed Social Security benefits cost the country more each year. To make matters worse, Congress voted to index payments for several major entitlement programs, saddling future generations with rising payments to millions of recipients. As the national debt increased, the annual interest payments on that debt grew as well, making it increasingly difficult to cut the deficit as time passed. In four years, Carter's deficits totaled $227 billion – more than Johnson, Nixon, and Ford combined. At the end of his term, the national debt stood at a staggering $930 billion.

Ronald Reagan ✻

Ronald Reagan, a conservative Republican, attempted to reduce waste in the federal government by cutting non-essential government programs. While the notion was a good one, the cuts amounted to a drop in the bucket compared to what Reagan was spending on the military during the cold war's arms race. Instead of raising money by increasing taxes, however, Reagan's plan was to cut taxes, just as Kennedy had done.

The theory, called supply side economics, was simple: lower taxes on the wealthy so that they will invest their savings in the economy. After all, no one would deny that businesses would utilize the money more efficiently than the federal government. Reagan cut the top marginal tax rate from 70 percent to 50 percent in 1981. As hoped for, total tax revenues rose. However, the amounts collected were not enough to match what the government was spending. For every additional tax dollar taken in, Reagan spent $1.21. In the final analysis, Reagan created monstrous budget deficits eight years in a row. By the end of his term, he had added another $1.34 trillion to the national debt.

George Bush, Sr. ✻

The senior Bush inherited the accumulated debt burden of the prior administration. He found that interest costs on the national debt were increasing every year. Entitlement programs were also costing more also. Although he ran for office on a platform based on no new taxes, he soon realized that the country badly needed revenue and reversed his position. Even after raising taxes, which may have contributed to edging the country into a recession, the deficits continued to rise. Each year under his administration, the deficits grew larger. In only four years, Bush added an additional $933 billion to our national debt.

Bill Clinton ✻✻✻✻

Clinton recognized the dangers of the national debt problem and immediately raised taxes. Clinton was more fortunate than the senior Bush, however, in that the economy was already in an upswing. The growing economy made his tax increase more effective. Unlike other presidents, who cut taxes but spent even more money, Clinton was the first president to raise taxes and at the same time cut the budget. Can you imagine a Democratic president cutting welfare, food stamps, and other entitlement programs? Despite political heat from his party, that is exactly what Clinton did when, in 1994, he worked with a Republican Congress to attempt to reduce government spending and balance the budget.

Because of increased tax revenues and decreased spending, Clinton made continual progress getting America's financial house back in order. From 1993 to 1997, the budget deficits shrank each year. In 1998, for the first time in twenty-eight years, Clinton did what Ford, Carter, Reagan, and Bush failed to do: balance the budget. In fact, not only did he balance the budget in 1998, he also created a budget surplus of $69 billion. In 1999, the surplus was $125 billion and, in the year 2000, the government actually brought in $236 billion more than it spent. That year, we paid down our national debt by $223 billion. Clinton was the first president to not only recognize the dangers of the national debt but risk his own popularity to do something about it.

George W. Bush ✳

George W. Bush took office in 2001. Some presidents manage to take office at just the right time in the economic cycle, while others walk into a mess. In Bush's case, it was the latter. His administration inherited a crashing stock market, which augured an imminent recession.

To avert that possibility, Alan Greenspan, the chairman of the Federal Reserve, acted quickly and began cutting interest rates in January of 2001. The country slipped into recession just two months later. In September of that year, terrorists attacked the World Trade Center. National security became an important issue. Even within our country, corporate scandals threatened our financial system. Without a doubt, Bush had a lot on his plate. It is hard to know what policies he would have put in place had he not encountered those circumstances. What we do know is that the country elected Bush on a platform of fiscal conservatism and got anything but that.

Shortly after Bush took office, the Congressional Budget Office (CBO) projected that between 2002 and 2011, our budget surpluses would total some $5.6 trillion. Before leaving office, Clinton had laid out a plan to use the windfall to eliminate the national debt, which stood at $3.6 trillion. The government would use any additional monies to shore up Social Security and Medicare. Bush had different ideas. For some reason, he believed that the $5.6 trillion that the CBO said was coming in was actually his money to spend, even though government economists expected only $1.5 trillion to come in during his term in office.

Bush enacted two large tax cuts, purportedly to stimulate the economy. Given that corporate tax revenues were already off by twenty percent because of the recession, many questioned whether the country could afford the tax cuts. Others questioned why the tax cuts mainly benefited the rich. Studies have shown that if you want to give the economy a quick fix, you give the tax cuts to lower income workers who will spend it quickly. Those in higher brackets are much more apt to save the money, which does nothing to stimulate the economy in the near term. Therefore, it would be difficult to argue that the sole purpose of the cuts was to stimulate the economy.

In retrospect, the tax cuts did little to stimulate the economy. The recession and the terrorist attacks had people so worried about the future that many squirreled the money away for a rainy day. As tax revenues decreased and expenditures increased, the budget surplus quickly evaporated. The 2000 surplus of $236 billion dwindled to a $127 billion surplus in 2001. Bush reversed an eight-year trend of lower budget deficits.

By 2002, the budget surplus had turned into a budget deficit totaling $157 billion. Our national debt, which the government was supposed to pay off in ten years, once again grew bigger. The CBO revised their estimates and claimed that their prior estimate of $5.6 trillion in surpluses, predicted just a year earlier, was likely to be off by about $4 trillion. As to why, they blamed the recession, tax cuts, and increased government spending.

Was there a method to Bush's madness? Some say that Bush knew exactly what he was doing but feared public outcry if he revealed his plan too soon. Bush wanted to reduce taxes drastically over time, especially taxes on the rich so that corporate America would benefit. The plan also encouraged savings for the same purpose. If corporations received more capital, they would buy more equipment, become more productive, and hire more workers. Everyone would be happy, or so the theory went.

In four years, Bush added $926 billion to the national debt. In the eight years that the two Bushes were in office, together they added $1.859 trillion to the national debt, almost six times as much as Clinton did during his eight years in office. Those statistics help to refute the common wisdom that portrays Republicans as fiscal conservatives and Democrats as spendthrifts.

Bush had an agenda beyond helping to create a stronger economy. Bush also wanted re-election, and that created a huge conflict of interest. Bush targeted retirees by passing the prescription drug plan for Medicare. Programs like this, as well as the already implemented tax cuts, benefited Bush's re-election efforts because it is very difficult for the opposition to campaign on a platform of taking money away from the electorate. Unfortunately, because these spending programs are grandfathered in, they will continue to add to the national debt. As the national debt grows, the interest payments on that debt add even more to the annual budget deficit. So where do we go from here?

The Path of Least Resistance

When a government's debt gets too high, their first course of action is to try to borrow money from other countries. We have been doing that for quite some time. When our government needs money, it issues bonds and notes. Foreign investors purchase much of our debt; Japan and China are the biggest buyers.

When U.S. interest rates are low and the value of the U.S. dollar is declining, our debt does not look like a very good investment. If the dollar declines while foreigners hold our debt, they lose money when they eventually must convert their investment proceeds into their own currency. Thus, without offering much higher interest rates, a declining dollar jeopardizes our ability to attract foreign investors.

Figure 2.1 — National Debt from 1940 to present

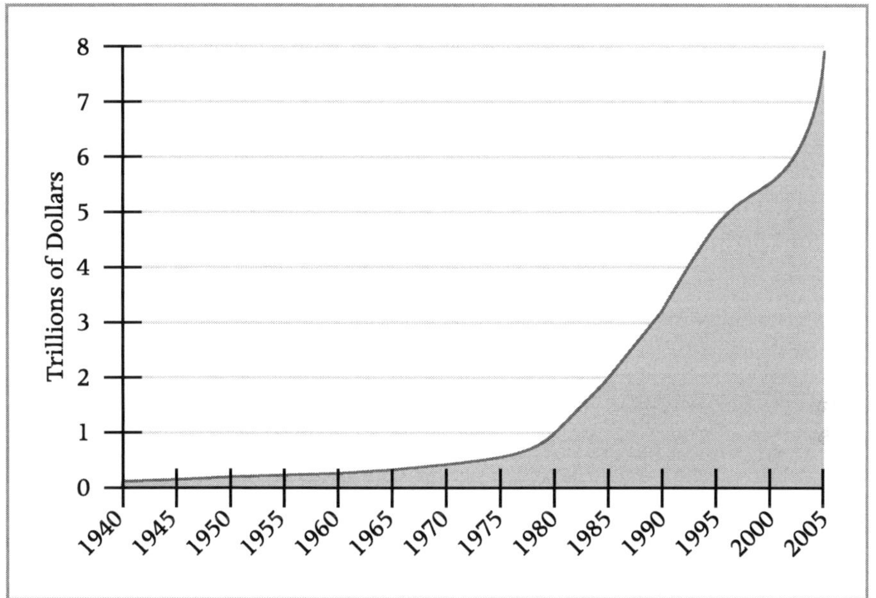

A second course of action for a government is to implement an austerity budget and raise taxes to bring in revenues. We have discussed why that is politically unfeasible. The entitlement programs, put in place by Johnson and augmented by various presidents along the way, have grown too big. They act as an inoperable cancer on the economy. If the government raises taxes, the additional revenues would amount to a drop in the bucket and could have even worse effects on the economy.

The third course of action is to monetize the debt. That simply means that the government increases the money supply so that is has more dollars to repay the debt. You may remember that Germany attempted the same tactic to repay its post-war debts, with disastrous results. Both Brazil and Argentina tried to do the same thing, only to ignite hyperinflations. In fact, every nation that ever inflated their currency eventually regretted it. Why then, you might argue, would our country ever resort to that?

Well, you can see that the government has only three options:

1. Borrow money.
2. Reduce spending and raise taxes.
3. Monetize the debt (print money).

Politicians typically believe that, instead of borrowing money, it would be much simpler just to print more. Governments whose currency is not pegged to a commodity such as gold have the license to do that and, invariably, that is what they do. Let us assume that they decide to double the current money supply. There are now twice as many dollars in circulation, although the number of goods and services has not increased.

In that scenario, the price of all goods and services would soon double. What happens to the government's debt? It is cut in half. As a by-product, the economy is also in high gear because that extra money works like a shot of adrenaline. Instantly, everyone has more money. Companies invest in new capital equipment and hire more employees. Everyone is happy and the politicians all get re-elected.

As we have seen time and time again, however, nothing really changes. The government will continue to overspend and the economy will be like a junkie hooked on credit. The fix from the increased money supply is only temporary. The increased money supply leads to inflation, which leads to higher interest rates. The government now has to pay even more to borrow money. Once again, the "easy" solution is to print a little more money. No politician will face the alternative — austerity — because recessions and depressions are politically unpopular.

As you can see, the budget deficit is a crisis because our government simply does not bring in enough revenue to fund ongoing expenditures. Each time the government runs an annual budget deficit, the total budget deficit grows larger. Could things get any worse? What else could cause the government to need even more money than they are already spending?

Ticking Time Bomb #2 ~
The Social Security and Medicare Crises

Franklin D. Roosevelt signed the Social Security Act into law in 1935. The country was still struggling with the Depression, and poverty was rampant. We needed a way to protect the elderly poor. Because the life expectancy for men was only sixty-seven years, the government anticipated paying benefits, beginning at age sixty-five, to only a small percentage of the population and for only a few years.

The initial tax burden on workers was a miniscule 2 percent — hardly enough for anyone to complain about given the altruistic results achieved. As the years went by, however, two trends combined that required workers to pay an ever-increasing portion of their wages into the Social Security "trust fund."

The first trend was the longevity of retirees – better healthcare began to add years to their life expectancies, resulting in a longer payout period for each retiree. The second trend, somewhat related to the first, was a change in the ratio of workers to retirees. Each year more and more workers would enter the retiree camp and live longer, while the number of workers supporting them lagged behind proportionately. For example, in the 1930s there were forty-five workers for every one retiree collecting Social Security; by 1950 there were only sixteen, and by 2003, there were only three.

The Empty Cookie Jar

Along the way, the government led the public to believe that their contributions were going into an account, which the government would use to pay them when they retired. That was the original idea. Before long, politicians decided that it would be all right to use the money for other purposes as long as they issued IOUs so that future politicians realized that the government owed money to the Social Security trust fund. The great benefit to the politicians was that they could overspend, take the money they needed from the trust fund, and not have to report the borrowed funds as part of the budget deficit.

As the years went by, Congress passed amendments to the original Social Security Act that greatly expanded the benefits received. The first major change came in 1939, when Congress, in addition to providing coverage for the retirees themselves, extended coverage to their dependents and survivors as well. In 1957, Congress extended benefits to the disabled. In 1966, it took in Medicare and Medicaid under the Social Security umbrella.

By 1968, the government had no choice but to increase the combined employer/employee tax to 8 percent to cover the additional expense. By 1982, even more retirees were entering the pool, and the system was once again losing money. In 1990, Congress increased the payroll tax again, this time to 15.3 percent of the first $55,200 of earnings. To squeeze even more money from the system, the government started taxing the benefits paid to the retirees.

The increased taxes did bring in close to $2 trillion over a twenty-year period, which would have been great if it had gone into the fund. As has always been the case, however, the government spent the money and replaced it with IOUs.

As late as 2003, Social Security actually brought in a surplus of $161 billion. That left the system with $3.5 trillion in the fund. However, as explained, most of that was in the form of IOUs. Even if the government did pay back all the IOUs, they would still come up short. It is already committed to paying $14 trillion to future beneficiaries. The shortfall is a staggering $10.5 trillion.

In 1999, the government examined the rate of return provided in the stock market from 1946 to 1995 and concluded that if workers contributed 9.25 percent of their wages into private accounts, they would save more than enough for a comfortable retirement. However, the study assumes that we start with a clean slate. If that were the case, it might be possible for workers who are twenty-five years old now to fund their own retirement. However, that does not solve the problem of the $14 trillion that the government already owes to 77 million baby boomers who will begin collecting their benefits in just a few years. Those workers will not have time to benefit from the new system. Curiously, no one was willing to address that issue. Of course, after the Standard & Poor's 500 lost half of its value over the following two years, many questioned the plan's wisdom.

When the country re-elected Bush in 2004, he pledged to make the privatization of Social Security the centerpiece of an overhaul of the retirement system. However, setting up personal accounts will require the government to make up the difference to retirees from funds that normally would have come from payroll taxes. Therefore, to implement the program, the government will need to borrow the extra money, thus increasing the deficit even further. Given that the growing government deficit is already a concern, many argue that now is not the time for the government to go even further in debt.

The truth is that it's too late to fix the Social Security system; the government owes $14 trillion to baby boomers.

Social Security is a political hot potato and it will only get hotter. The current administration, the Congressional Budget Office, and the Social Security trustees have all obfuscated the truth about the state of the Social Security system. Bush has repeatedly misled the public by claiming that we are running a surplus. The Congressional Budget Office has ignored its own advisors' studies on generational accounting. (Generational accounting seeks to determine what burden our current spending and accumulated debt place on future generations.) The Social Security trustees have repeatedly underestimated the problem, including failing to account for the fact that new retirees are expected to live four years longer on average.

The facts are clear: the current system promises today's workers that future generations will support them, just as today's workers are currently supporting today's retirees. Demographic studies have clearly proved that the system cannot go forward under those assumptions. As to the $14 trillion owed to 77 million Boomers, someone, somewhere, somehow will need to pay that bill. Because it is future debt, it does not show up in the national debt. How many ways can you think of to pay a $14 trillion debt? If you have been paying attention, you might want to take a stab at it: print money.

An 800-pound Gorilla

Does the Social Security problem worry you? It should. Unfortunately, it pales in comparison to the Medicare situation. As you may remember, President Johnson signed the Medicare bill into law in 1965. Like Social Security, no one would argue with Medicare's good intent. However, at the time no one could have projected how expensive it would become. Who would have predicted the extent of medical cost increases, which have resulted from new, expensive technologies, or how much life expectancy would increase, or how the increasing costs would fall upon a diminishing ratio of workers to retirees?

The new drug prescription plan will also place a severe strain on Medicare. While originally purported to cost $400 billion over the next ten years, the administration later admitted it would cost $534 billion. As more benefits phase in, the following ten years will cost close to $1 trillion. Even those estimates may be low. The important thing to remember is that those costs are entirely unfunded. There is no money to pay for this – unless, of course, we look to our children.

When Congress originally created Medicare, the typical recipient was a low-income, elderly person hospitalized for surgery. Today the elderly are far more expensive to treat. Many have chronic ailments that require continuous doctor visits. Almost half will require nursing home care, many suffering from dementia. In summary, the drugs and services required to treat the elderly are extremely expensive and rising daily. We have no money to pay for it. Our politicians are shifting this enormous debt burden on to our children.

Medicaid is a government program that provides medical benefits for America's poor. After Social Security and Medicare, Medicaid is the most expensive welfare program. The spending on Medicaid, however, has even outpaced that of Medicare during the past few years. Much of Medicaid's expenditures go to provide nursing homes for the elderly. As we know, as the number of seniors increase and their life expectancies lengthen, the cost of nursing home care for this group will escalate as well.

The Fiscal Gap

Social Security, Medicare, and Medicaid: What do the expenditures actually mean going forward and how can we pay for them? To find out, in 2002, the secretary of the treasury commissioned a study. The idea was rather simple. If we can project the costs going forward and do the same with expected revenues from payroll taxes, we can determine how much of a shortfall we will have. Knowing this, we can then determine how much extra money we will need to fund the programs. Because most baby boomers will be about halfway through their old age in 2030, the analysts chose that date as the cutoff.

By making certain calculations, we can also determine what the actual shortage is at this moment in time. In other words, given the assumption that payroll taxes would remain the same, how much would we need to keep these programs running?

Once the study provided that number (called the fiscal gap), the government realized the extent of its true debt. Are you ready? The fiscal gap — again, the amount of money we would need today to ensure our seniors will receive their Social Security checks and Medicare benefits now amounts to $45 trillion. To put that number in perspective, if everyone in the country calculated their net worth and sent the government a check for that amount, it would only total $40 trillion. That means that the country does not have enough money to fund entitlement programs and will need to print more money.

Imagine that your bills were increasing each year but your salary was decreasing each year. That's the position our government is now in. The government's bills (Social Security and Medicare) will skyrocket as boomers retire. Meanwhile, the amount the government receives in payroll taxes will remain the same or even decline because of proportionately fewer workers in the younger generation.

It is only a matter of time before other economists begin to realize the severity of the government's economic crisis. It is a fait accompli that our politicians, Democrat or Republican, will not risk political suicide by recommending either severe cutbacks to the big three entitlement programs or a sharp increase in taxes. The former is not politically feasible and the latter is not economically feasible (a severe depression would result).

Soon, bond investors will come to the same conclusion and, fearing inflation, they will demand a much higher rate of interest to encourage them to buy government debt. Higher interest rates will cause a slowdown in the economy as investors, who might have invested in stocks, buy bonds instead.

The government will print money to keep the economy from stalling. The added liquidity will produce inflation, which will cause the dollar to decline in value relative to other major currencies. A lower dollar will result in higher costs of imports from countries such as Japan whose currency floats free against the dollar. The higher costs of those goods will add to the inflation.

Unless the government prints more money, both the federal and state governments will have no choice but to raise taxes to pay their bills. If that happens, workers will witness their real wages falling progressively as taxes eat up a growing percentage of their paychecks. Lower real wages will trigger a chain of economic events. Workers will have less money to spend and less money to invest. They will buy less, so businesses will produce less. Businesses will lay off workers and unemployed workers will file for unemployment insurance and Medicaid benefits. The government will need even more money. To get it, they will have no other choice but to print it.

We have now examined two of the seven geopolitical crises that will contribute to the perfect financial storm and promote future inflation. They are:

1. The budget deficit
2. The Social Security and Medicare crises

The third geopolitical crisis could be averted if the government chose to take decisive action. But will they?

Ticking Time Bomb #3 ~ The Healthcare Crisis

The healthcare system in the United States has fallen and it can't get up. It's becoming more expensive every day. Because of that, healthcare is a potent factor shrinking your money. You pay for healthcare even if you never see a doctor. You pay because your insurance becomes more expensive; you pay because your taxes increase; and you pay because your employer is less profitable.

Since 1965, after adjusting for inflation, the cost of healthcare has quadrupled. On an annual basis, costs have risen at twice the rate of inflation during that same time period. If healthcare costs had simply grown in line with the economy, we would be spending only half as much on healthcare as we do today.

While we can attribute the rising costs of healthcare to several factors, the aging of the population — a trend that we cannot control — is the primary driver. Older people require much more healthcare than younger people do. In fact, on a per capita basis, healthcare costs for those over sixty-five are nearly five times as much as for those under sixty-five. As more and more people cross over into old age, we can expect the total dollars that we spend on healthcare as a nation to explode.

Until the late 1990s, company plans insulated many workers from the rising costs of health insurance. As healthcare costs rose, however, employers insisted that employees share some of the cost. Initially, employee coverage dropped from 100 percent to 90 percent, then to 80 percent. With the size of today's medical bills, even 20 percent of a very large number is enough to bankrupt many families.

The World Health Organization ranks the U.S. healthcare system thirty-seventh in the world. Nearly all other industrialized countries have better healthcare systems, healthier citizens, and pay less for their healthcare. Can you guess why? It is because they have nationalized healthcare systems.

We spend 50 percent more on healthcare than any other developed nation. Because half of the total amount of healthcare costs comes from public taxes, the healthcare system is definitely your problem. What do we get for our money? As a whole, Americans are the most uninsured and underinsured in the developed world – our healthcare system leaves over 45 million people without health insurance and thus vulnerable to financial ruin. Moreover, our citizens are less healthy than those in Europe, Canada, or Japan. In infant mortality, we rank twenty-third in the world; in life expectancy, we rank twentieth for women and twenty-first for men.

The Underlying Problem

Our healthcare system is based on a third-party-payer financial system. What that means is that you, the end user, do not pay for the service. Instead, a third party, the insurance company, stands between you and your doctor, the service provider. While your goal is to receive the best service, your insurance company's goal is to pay the least amount possible for the service. Your doctor finds himself caught in the middle because cost constraints imposed by the insurance company prevent him from providing quality care. This kind of system maximizes unhappiness and guarantees conflict.

The bureaucracy in healthcare also adds to your costs. In recent years, the American healthcare system has added two to three administrative workers to the system for every additional doctor. We all have to pay for underwriting, sales representatives, advertising, claims adjusters, and claims administrators. How much does this bureaucracy cost us? Estimates run between 18 and 24 percent of our healthcare dollar, in comparison to other countries that average around 10 percent.

The Fox in the Henhouse

Prescription drugs are one of the largest and fastest growing segments of the healthcare industry. According to the Centers for Disease Control (CDC), in 1980 we spent $12 billion on prescription drugs. Now we spend nearly $200 billion, and our cost for drugs is increasing at 12 percent a year.

In 1980, spending on drugs accounted for almost 5 percent of total healthcare costs. It has more than doubled, and it is expected to triple within a few years. The facts are that people take more drugs than they used to, newer drugs are more expensive, and drug companies price popular drugs at whatever the market will bear. The growth in drug sales correlates to the marketing efforts of the major pharmaceutical companies who are unabashedly selling us more drugs, many of which we are required to take for longer periods. Drugs for cholesterol, high blood pressure, and even depression all fall into that category. Take them for life and call me in the morning. You'll need it because big pharma is shrinking your money by increasing prices at four times the rate of inflation.

We all know that prescription drugs are expensive. However, not everyone knows that, in the United States, we pay from 30 percent to 60 percent more than everyone else in the industrialized world does for the very same drug. What is going on? The fact is that pharmaceutical companies charge whatever the market will bear.

In countries with nationalized medicine, the country negotiates with the drug companies to pay a reasonable price. In our country, Congress allows pharmaceutical companies to charge whatever they want, which makes some drugs too costly for many citizens. To make matters worse,

Congress forbids Medicare from negotiating with pharmaceutical companies to obtain a lower price. Thus, all Americans must pay the inflated costs through higher taxes. You would almost think that Congress listens to big pharma more than it listens to you and me.

The pharmaceutical industry is the most profitable industry in the country. Given that employers must pay larger premiums to health insurers to pay for the higher price of drugs, big pharma has siphoned off a part of the earnings of all corporate America. When employers cut back on health benefits, the public will bear even more of the burden of overpriced pharmaceuticals than they do now.

Code Blue

In looking at the entire healthcare industry, we can see that it is a fragmented assortment of profit-driven entities, not one of which speaks for what is best for American healthcare overall. The costs of prescription drugs and health insurance premiums are in unsustainable, upward spirals. The consumer is absorbing the costs, either directly or indirectly through taxes. Even now, the present healthcare system does not adequately serve our country. As our population ages, the additional demands on the system will be enormous.

Drug companies, insurance companies, and profit-hungry hospitals have successfully scared the public into believing that nationalized medicine is "big government." However, numerous studies have shown that a single-payer system can restrain costs and provide quality healthcare. The fundamental problems with the third-party-payer system we have now cause Americans' healthcare costs to be almost double those in other countries.

In terms of administrative costs, Medicare, which is a single-payer system, is the most efficiently run healthcare system in America. While Medicare's administrative costs average two percent, the administrative costs of private insurers run between 12 percent and 30 percent. The reason Medicare's costs are lower is because it provides standardized, universal coverage, whereas private insurance encompasses thousands of plans and providers, requiring an army of administrators whose primary job is to deny claims.

The rising cost of healthcare in the United States is destined to continue to shrink your money unless or until the United States implements a national healthcare program. Given that such a policy shift is not imminent, you should not count on an end to the trend of rising healthcare costs any time soon. If you are young, expect the government to take more out of your paycheck to provide for the costs. If you have employer sponsored health insurance, expect your participation to increase, your deductibles to rise, and your co-pays to increase.

Business leaders predict that health insurance premiums will rise 17 percent per year over the next five years. For the most part, employers will pass on the greater part of those increases to employees. Therefore, you may find that the additional cost of health insurance will entirely negate standard cost-of-living increases.

We all share the costs of healthcare through either increased insurance premiums or increased taxes, so the rising cost of healthcare is everybody's problem. However, politicians have not addressed our country's future healthcare needs or the consequences of the costs. The aggregate costs will act as an anchor that will slow the economy and reduce standards of living in the years ahead. Any factor that slows the economy may induce the government to inflate the money supply in order to avoid recession. Such an expansion, as we have learned, would shrink your money.

We have now examined the first three of the seven geopolitical crises that will contribute to the perfect financial storm and promote future inflation. They are:

1. The budget deficit
2. The Social Security and Medicare crises
3. The healthcare crisis

Next we'll examine what may be the most important of all seven crises.

Ticking Time Bomb #4 ~ The Trade Deficit

In the 1960s, America began leaking money like a twenty-year-old Oldsmobile leaks oil. Globalization was the cause. Of course, nobody used that term in those days. Nevertheless, large corporations—soon to be known as multinationals—began expanding abroad. They spent millions of dollars overseas – dollars that otherwise would have been spent at home.

Soon those foreign countries found themselves awash in dollars. After a while, they wanted to exchange a portion of their dollars for gold. The United States had previously signed the Bretton Woods Agreement, promising to allow foreign governments to redeem dollars for gold at a rate of $35 for each ounce of gold. Before long, however, the country began running low on gold reserves. As a result, in 1971, Richard Nixon declared that we would no longer honor our promise to exchange gold for foreign currencies.

In 1973, after Nixon closed the gold window, all countries agreed to let their currencies float freely against one another, allowing the laws of supply and demand to determine their value. Prior to 1973, all currencies were pegged to the dollar, which, in turn, was pegged to a predetermined price for gold. The new system, thus, is a rather recent experiment, especially when observed from a longer-term historical perspective.

For more than three decades, the United States has benefited greatly from the new system. After cutting the dollar loose from the gold peg, it could buy whatever it liked from the rest of the world using dollars that it could print at will. Given that license, the United States ran trade deficits year in and year out. (The annual trade deficit shows the difference between the amount of money we spent on imports versus the amount of money earned from exports during the past year.)

Over the years, we have purchased trillions of dollars worth of goods from the rest of the world, oblivious to future consequences. However, as we will learn later in this chapter, the chickens are about to come home to roost. Nixon's decision to close the gold window may yet give rise to enormous global hardship.

The U.S. Predicament

When a country exports more goods than it imports, it creates a trade surplus. Conversely, when it imports more than it exports, it creates a trade deficit. Either way, trade imbalances can cause problems.

At first blush, you might expect that a trade surplus would be a good thing. However, whenever money comes into a country, it can distort the economy, eventually producing a boom and bust cycle. History is replete with examples. The genesis of the great crash in 1929 was the large amount of gold that England and France sent to America to pay for arms for World War I.

More recently, countries in Asia suffered boom and bust cycles. In the 1980s, Japan's enormous trade surplus fostered a boom and subsequent bust of both their stock and real estate markets. When the bubble burst, the stock market lost 75 percent of its value and real estate market valuations were cut in half. In the 1990s, capital migrating from Japan in search of cheaper labor infected Asian markets. As the money poured in, their stock markets soared. Thailand's share prices quadrupled between 1988 and 1993, while property prices rose as much as 1000 percent. When their stock market crashed, it lost 95 percent of its value.

When money gushes into a country, productive enterprises cannot immediately absorb it. Instead, it sloshes through the system causing inflation, often disguised as asset bubbles, which eventually pop. It is not necessary for a government to print money for their money supply to expand. All that is necessary is that it accepts money from outside its borders.

Both China and Japan run large trade surpluses against the United States today and are well aware of this problem. They face another conundrum. If they convert the excess dollars to their own currency, the value of their currency will rise in relation to the value of the dollar, making their exports less competitive with American goods. In effect, their trade success becomes self-limiting – they shoot themselves in the foot if they convert the dollars to their own currency and spend the money in their own country.

Until now, the only solution for both Japan and China has been to invest the dollars back in the United States so as not to adversely affect their trade advantage and upset their economies. Their primary way of doing this has been to buy U.S. government bonds and other federal debt; but they also buy stocks, corporate bonds, and sometimes make direct investments in real estate. At last count, their investments totaled over $4 trillion dollars. Moreover, because the majority of their invest-

Figure 2.2 — Trade balance 1990 – 2005

ments have been in government bonds, we owe both countries a great deal of money. Still, we keep borrowing.

A Reckoning Awaits

Foreigners mock our moral fiber and claim that we have become a non-productive society that primarily values consumption and luxuries. Are they right? It would be difficult to argue the point. In 1950, we produced more than half of the world's goods; now we only produce about one-quarter. We have run trade deficits for thirty years in a row. Moreover, we are the world's largest debtor by a large margin. Are there consequences?

The United States will never be able to manufacture most products as cheaply as it can buy them from overseas manufacturers. Therefore, we can expect the trade deficit to continue to worsen. The following balance of payments graph shows how the cumulative trade deficit has grown over the past fifteen years.

We also know that we cannot depend on foreign governments to finance our spending habits forever. Foreign governments are very much aware of the potential risks they face. The larger our overall debt grows, the less likely we will be able to pay it back. If we do not have enough money to pay our debts — which include ongoing interest payments, principal repayments as notes and bonds mature, and guaranteed entitlement payments — we may have no other choice but to print money. If we print money, inflation will rise and the value of the dollar will fall. Foreign investors thus risk repayment in depreciated dollars.

When U.S. dollars come back into the United States from foreign investors, those dollars generally find their way into the banking system. Because banks can lend a multiple of what they hold in reserve, the inflow of dollars provides an ongoing dose of credit to our economy, which shows up in the money supply. This trend, beginning in the early 1980s, accelerated in the early 1990s and spawned the stock market boom. In the last few years, foreign buying of government agency bonds from Fannie Mae and Freddie Mac made the real estate boom possible.

The data is clear that the money coming in from foreign dollars is not going to productive investment. The government is using the money to pay interest on prior debts, while households are spending the money on current consumption. That is clearly not a good sign.

Going forward, we must ask ourselves what possible scenarios could result if foreign lenders decide to take their dollar holdings elsewhere. Let me propose a hypothetical scenario. Assume Japan decides not to invest in our treasury and agency debt. Instead, it buys Eurodollars. The dollar would fall against the Euro. Because oil is priced in dollars, OPEC would either raise their price to compensate for their foreign exchange losses (it has already done this once) or reprice oil in Euros. In either case, much higher oil prices would occur, with attendant inflationary pressures.

Because all commodities are priced in dollars, commodity prices would rise as well. Rising commodity prices add to inflationary pressures. A lower dollar would cause bondholders to sell, rather than risk payback in depreciated dollars. When the bond market declines, long-term interest rates rise as they maintain an inverse relationship. When corporations must pay more to borrow, they must also raise prices to protect their profit margins. That is also inflationary.

The Fed Will Fight Back

If this scenario were to occur, the U.S. economy would begin to slide into a severe recession. While businesses may attempt to raise prices to compensate for their increased borrowing costs, demand for their goods and services will simply not exist. They will begin slashing prices and reducing overhead by eliminating workers. Prices could then succumb to the worldwide deflation that will eventually get the upper hand.

However, the United States government will not go down without a fight. While deflationists make a very strong case, the fact of the matter is that the Federal Reserve will simply not allow deflation, which would lead to depression. They have made that perfectly clear. In 2002, the board of governors circulated the following paper entitled, "Preventing Deflation: Lessons from Japan's Experience in the 1990s."

> *Based on all these considerations, we draw the general lesson from Japan's experience that when inflation and interest rates have fallen close to zero, and the risk of deflation is high, stimulus — both monetary and fiscal — should go beyond the levels conventionally implied by baseline forecasts of future inflation and economic activity.*[1]

According to this paper, the board of governors is well aware of the potential economic implications of a sustained deflationary slump and wants to avoid that at all costs. They believe that it was the Japanese's "failure to provide sufficient stimulus to maintain growth and positive inflation" that resulted in Japan's depression. They further state that once inflation and short-term interest rates approach zero, both monetary and fiscal policy should go beyond conventional levels, which means that the government is prepared to fight deflation by any means possible. That would likely include both fiscal stimulus (government spending programs) and monetary stimulus (printing money).

What effects would fiscal and monetary stimulus have on the economy? As we have seen, when additional money comes into an economy, it always has an inflationary effect, with a lag that can sometimes be as much as two years. Unfortunately, the benefits of monetary stimulus are not as great as they once were.

Pushing on a String

The U.S economy is no longer capable of dancing to the tune of monetary stimulus. Less and less productive, it is like a boxer well past his prime. Moreover, it is weighed down by debt and it adds more each year. As the total debt grows, interest payments take a larger share of the gross domestic product (GDP). Going forward, inflation-adjusted entitlement programs alone are destined to bankrupt the country. Meanwhile, politicians continue to do what politicians do best: dole out benefits to the electorate in order to gain votes. It does not take a genius to see that America has lost its way.

A small dose of monetary stimulus, the most likely first strike the Fed will take, will not be enough to revive the economy. Here is why: in a normal economy, businesses would use that money to expand their plants and modernize their equipment, thereby increasing productivity and output. However, this time will be different. Manufacturing has made a grand exodus offshore in search of cheap labor. As a result, the country already suffers from overcapacity in its factories. The next time businesses get cheap money from the Fed, they are more likely to pay down debt or invest in overseas operations rather than invest in new plants and equipment in the United States.

What will consumers do with new cash? In prior periods of monetary stimulus, the consumer would use those extra dollars to buy products from U.S. factories. In today's economy, however, consumers are more likely to pay down personal debts to relieve the stress caused by monthly bills exceeding income. In addition, many of the products they do purchase will be imports, worsening the current account deficit even further.

In short, here's why monetary stimulus may not have the desired effect.

1. Businesses and consumers are more heavily in debt than ever before, and they will use the money to pay down debts.

Figure 2.3 — Money Supply (M3)

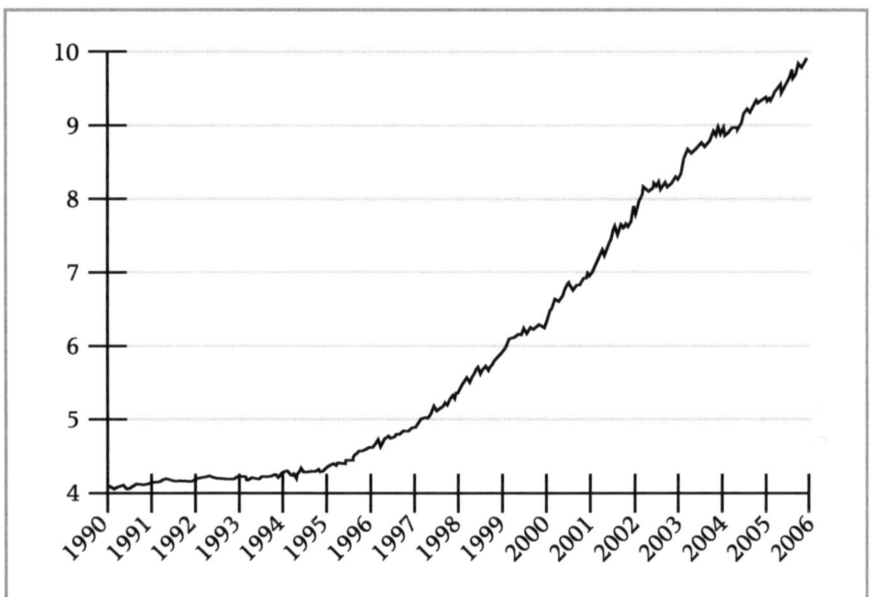

2. The money will leak out of the country by businesses that will invest overseas and consumers who will buy more competitively priced items from Asia.

Money is also likely to chase existing and new asset bubbles. Is there any proof that future monetary stimulus will not be as effective as it once was? Yes. We have already received a healthy dose of monetary stimulus from foreigners who took the dollars we sent them for imports and invested them back into our country. The money went into banks and fostered credit creation. That is no different from the Fed creating credit by printing money or using any of its other tools to stimulate the economy. Figure 2.3 is a chart on M3 (the broadest measure of money supply), showing the expansion in money supply that resulted.

Eventually the economy will begin to slow because it is fundamentally unsound. When that happens, expect the Federal Reserve to implement an initial stimulus package. After the initial stimulus fails to bring the desired result, it is unlikely that the Fed will do nothing more and allow the economy to falter. Instead, they will more than likely point to some benefits gained from the first stimulus package as justification for a second.

One thing we can count on is that the amount of monetary stimulus required to keep the economy afloat will create tremendous dislocation in markets, possibly spawning asset bubbles and strong trends in physical commodities and tangibles. This financial storm will make some people richer and others poorer. The time to make money will be short, however. Your best course of action will be to learn how to use various investment vehicles and take action. We will discuss exactly how to do that in part 2 of this book.

What you have just learned about the fundamental unsoundness of our economy and what the Federal Reserve will need to do to prevent a severe recession, may be the best reasons to expect future inflation. However, even if the economy had no structural problems, we could expect the crises discussed in this book to add to inflationary pressures.

We have now examined the first four of the seven geopolitical crises that will contribute to the perfect financial storm and promote future inflation. They are:
1. The budget crisis
2. The Social Security and Medicare crises
3. The healthcare crisis
4. The trade deficit

The next crisis, while a bane to most, offers the astute investor a number of ways to profit.

Ticking Time Bomb #5 ~ The Energy Crisis

Energy and progress go hand in hand. Manufacturing produces wealth but also requires energy. Without an abundant source of energy and the technology to harness it, progress and development cannot occur.

Oil will remain the world's leading source of energy for at least the next two decades and possibly longer. While natural gas, coal, and nuclear power can be used to generate electricity, only oil can power the world's transportation systems. Oil and its refined products account for

95 percent of the fuel consumed in cars, trucks, and airplanes. As the number of vehicles and airplanes increases, the amount of oil needed will increase as well.

America began consuming more oil than it produced in 1946. However, for the next fifteen years, its domestic shortfall caused little concern because its oil companies still controlled much of the flow of oil from the Middle East. Armed with their advanced technological know how, oil companies found they could dictate terms to the oil states. Eventually, however, the oil states became angry over what they considered exploitation of their natural resources.

In 1961, Venezuela, Iran, Iraq, Kuwait, and Saudi Arabia formed the Organization of Petroleum Exporting Countries (OPEC) in order to gain leverage over the oil companies. One by one, the oil states nationalized their oil, forcing the oil companies to accept reduced royalties. With more than half the world's oil under the control of OPEC, the cartel could control both pricing and supply.[2]

In 1971, oil production peaked in the United States. With each passing year, oil production fell and America grew more dependent on OPEC. By the mid-1970s, U.S. policymakers began to make plans for military intervention in the Middle East should it one day become necessary. In 1980, Jimmy Carter made it clear that America would use force against any adversary that might impede the flow of oil from the Persian Gulf. In what was later referred to as the Carter doctrine, he stated the following.

"Any attempt by any outside force to gain control of the Persian Gulf region will be regarded as an assault on the vital interests of the United States of America and will be repelled by any means necessary, including military force."[3]

Washington policymakers had proposed taking the Middle East by force as far back as 1975, but they lacked adequate justification to carry out their plans. The Iraq invasion of Kuwait gave them their first excuse to establish a beachhead. Even before the 9/11 attacks, Washington policymakers had been making plans about Iraq's oil. Analysts felt that, with the help of American oil companies, production could be doubled.

If Iraq could be convinced to leave OPEC, the additional oil would be enough to undermine OPEC 's ability to control prices. However, it would cost as much as $40 billion to rebuild Iraq's oil infrastructure. To get the major oil companies to make that investment, Washington would need to guarantee them a new regime friendly to America, military security, and a handsome share of the revenues.[4]

Washington believed that by controlling the Gulf and the Middle East, the United States could gain leverage over other countries that are dependent on Gulf oil for energy.[5] However, the United States is not the only player in the oil chess game. Both Russia and China are wooing Saudi Arabia. If Russia and Saudi Arabia combine forces, they would dominate a large portion of the world's energy supply. A China/Saudi marriage is not out of the question either. The Saudis clearly want the burgeoning Chinese market and China needs access to Saudi oil. One thing China has no shortage of is cash, and money talks in the world of oil.

Given the potential influence of Russia and China on Saudi Arabia, control of future Saudi oil by the United States is hardly a fait accompli. How the world energy map will eventually be redrawn remains unclear. Politics aside, the fundamentals of the energy crisis come down to supply and demand. Unfortunately, all evidence points to reduced supply and rising demand during the next two critical decades, before alternate fuels can lessen the world's dependency on oil.

Running on Fumes

Oil is a finite resource. Once the earth's supply is exhausted, humanity will find itself wholly dependent on other sources of energy. Since the 1950s, geologists have been trying to determine how much oil remains on the planet and, given estimates of expected usage, when we will reach the peak in production. Oil wells always produce far more in the early stages of their production, then progressively weaken as the oil becomes more difficult and expensive to extract. Knowing the peak in production (the point at which one-half of all supplies have been exhausted) is critical because that is when production begins to decline.

Once we reach the peak, the cost of energy is likely to skyrocket. Unfortunately, we will not know for sure when world oil production has peaked until after the fact, and by then it will be too late. Estimates range from as early as now to as late as 2018. The uncertainties arise from lack of good data on the reserves in the Middle East and Russia. The mean consensus, however, is that global oil production will peak about 2010.

In the 1950s, oil production in the United States increased every year. No one ever thought about running out of oil. No one, that is, except one renegade geologist who studied sophisticated mathematical models to find the answer. What M. King Hubbert discovered shocked the oil community and the world. Hubbert's models predicted that oil production in the United States would peak sometime in 1970. To nearly everyone's surprise, U.S. oil production did peak in 1971.

Years later, one of Hubbert's colleagues, Kenneth S. Deffeyes, employed the same methodology to attempt to determine when worldwide production would peak. Other geologists, employing Hubbert's principles, worked on the problem as well. All obtained similar results. While known reserves are relatively easy to calculate, the unknown reserves in the Middle East pose more of a problem. For that, we must examine the work of one of the world's foremost authorities on Middle East reserves, Dr. Colin Campbell.

Campbell is among the more pessimistic of the oil analysts and believes that world oil production is peaking now. He reminds us that the peak in discovery occurred in the 1960s and that the amount of oil discovered has fallen every year since. Moreover, Campbell claims that OPEC's estimates of Middle East oil reserves are grossly overstated. Further evidence that he is correct came in late 2005 when Farouk Al Zanki admitted to the world press that Kuwait's huge Burgan oil field (the second largest oil field in the world) has less oil remaining than was previously thought. Now, Al Zanki claims that the field's output, formerly projected to continue at 2 million barrels a day, will only be 1.7 million barrels.

In non-OPEC countries, known reserves have already peaked and are in rapid decline. Clearly, the United States must find its oil somewhere else. The politically sensitive Arctic National Wildlife Refuge is one place it is looking, but experts generally agree that output from that region would be inadequate to alter our dependency on OPEC. Additionally, most energy analysts believe that the large fields of oil have already been discovered; those that do remain will be harder to get to (lying deep beneath the sea or ice) and more costly to bring to production.

In summary, the supply of oil is running out faster than expected. The United States uses 25 percent of the world's oil, but produces only 2 percent. Non-OPEC oil is in decline, forcing OPEC to produce more. Moreover, OPEC reserves may be lower than official estimates. Finally, new oil exploration and production will be extremely expensive, adding to cost pressures.

Even if world demand remained constant, we would still run out of oil in the near future. However, that scenario is benign compared to reality. The fact is that world demand is rising even faster than analysts predicted just a few years ago. The next section explores the driving forces behind that demand.

The Hunger for Energy

Two components make up the rising demand for energy: a growing world population and the industrialization of developing countries. In just the last fifty years, the planet has added more than three billion people, doubling the population. Each year, 80 million more people inhabit the world. The world's population will reach 6.8 billion by 2010 and approach 8 billion by 2020.[6] More people require more energy.

The second component, the shift from agriculture to industry, is occurring in many parts of the world, such as China, India, and South America. Industry is extremely energy intensive: factories require energy, as does the transportation needed to ship final product. Industrialization also creates wealth, which creates an upward spiral of energy demand. A rise in manufacturing creates jobs, giving families more money to buy products, and that demand then leads to more manufacturing.

While we take electricity for granted, the majority of the world's population is still without it. Once they can afford it, they will want it. Once they have it, they will then want a stove, a refrigerator, a radio, and a TV set. Because the production and use of these products require such a great deal of energy, the global requirement for energy has consistently exceeded the rate of population growth.

China is gobbling up energy faster than any country on earth.

According to the U.S. Department of Energy, energy consumption in China will rise at roughly four times the rate in Europe and the United States at least through 2020. Other industrializing nations, such as India, Brazil, and Mexico, will exhibit a similar pattern. In short, a growing population coupled with a shift from agriculture to industry results in a rising demand for energy.

The Asian car market deserves special attention. Analysts expect the Chinese car market to expand at 15 to 20 percent per year over the next decade.[7] General Motors predicted that China would account for one-fifth of all new car sales between 2002 and 2012 — nearly twice as many as in the United States[8].

Hundreds of millions of Chinese see car ownership as a status symbol and a personal goal. Among urban Chinese, three-quarters plan to buy a car within the next five years. By all accounts, the Chinese car market is set to explode. A Nissan executive explained why: "An increasing number of people in China earn salaries equivalent to the price of a new car. As has happened in other markets, this is exactly the point in time when domestic car sales begin to take off."[9]

In other parts of Southeast Asia, where the middle class is slightly more developed, the number of cars on the road grows by 30 percent per year. In South Korea, the number of passenger cars quadrupled in only ten years, while gasoline consumption tripled. In India, with a middle class of 100 million, the number of cars tripled in the last decade and may triple again by 2020. Another 100 million consumers throughout the rest of Southeast Asia will soon be ready to buy cars as well.[10] As a result, demand for oil in these countries will *triple* in the next fifteen years. In the developing world, the future of China's energy usage is clear. They will emulate the United States, wanting bigger houses, bigger cars, and more appliances. They will also travel more. Witness the fact that air travel in China is growing at 20 percent per year and the government expects to add fifty passenger jets per year during the next twenty years.[11]

Before 1985, only 7 percent of Chinese homes had refrigerators; today that number is 75 percent. Households with TVs have climbed from 17 percent to 86 percent. The number of air conditioners has grown fifty-fold. Examples like these help to explain why power generation is one of the fastest-growing sectors of the developing world.[12] In fact, China has claimed that it will need to build sixty electric power plants each year for the next decade simply to keep up with demand.

Clearly, conventional estimates, both for the remaining supply of oil and the future demand for oil, have been far too conservative. The truth is we are running out of oil far more quickly than practically anyone expected. We are rapidly approaching an impasse where our energy-based global society will face an oil shock. Of course, the decisions politicians make regarding energy policy will play a large part in determining our fate.

The Politics of Energy

The future of energy is in the hands of governments. They can battle over the remaining drops of oil and natural gas on the planet or choose to implement conservation policies and marshal forces to free us from our dependence on carbon-based fuels. For three decades, the U.S. government has consistently made the wrong choices. When it mattered most, the United States turned its back on both conservation and the development of renewable energy sources, while catering to the whims of the oil and auto industries.

Meanwhile, countries almost entirely dependent on other nations for their energy needs — such as Japan, England, Germany, and Denmark — have pressed forward, both in conservation and in the development of new energy technologies. The Europeans lead the world in wind-power technology, while Japan excels in solar power.

Without radical policy changes at the highest levels of government, the focus will remain on the control and exploitation of remaining supplies of oil and natural gas. Renewable energy technologies will continue to improve, but without massive government funding and tax credits for research and development, those technologies will not play a significant role in meeting global energy needs for several decades at best.

Despite government efforts to control global oil and gas supplies, the energy crisis will worsen. Higher prices and increased volatility — by-products of supply uncertainty — will become the norm. In the final analysis, the politics of energy and those special interests that promote carbon-based technologies have delayed the inevitable transition to new, cleaner energy sources at the risk of both military conflict and future cataclysmic climate change.

We have now examined the first five of the seven geopolitical crises that will contribute to the perfect financial storm and promote future inflation. They are:

1. The budget deficit
2. The Social Security and Medicare crises
3. The healthcare crisis
4. The trade deficit
5. The energy crisis

In the next section, we will discuss an impending crisis that our government has tried its best to suppress.

Ticking Time Bomb #6 ~ Global Warming

Climate records confirm that our planet's atmosphere is warming. In fact, since 1990, temperatures have risen six times faster than during the past 250 years. Of the ten warmest years on record since 1860, eight have occurred since 1990.

Why is the climate warming more quickly? As far back as 1955, we knew the answer. At that time, Charles Keeling confirmed that carbon dioxide levels in the atmosphere had been rising since the mid-nineteenth century.[13] Prior to the mid-nineteenth century, the amount of carbon dioxide in the atmosphere had remained steady at 280 parts per million (PPM) for almost 10,000 years, which helped maintain the ideal climatic conditions that allowed civilizations to flourish.

377 PPM and Rising

With the age of industrialization, however, the burning of coal and oil released carbon dioxide into the atmosphere. When carbon dioxide builds up in the atmosphere, it traps the heat that otherwise would be reflected back into space. That heat expands the ocean water, which accelerates evaporation, allowing the water vapor to trap even more heat, thus warming the earth. Today, the level of carbon dioxide in the atmosphere stands at 377 PPM, the highest level in over 400,000 years.

In 1995, forty years after Keeling discovered a trend of rising carbon dioxide levels, a team of scientists at the National Ocean and Atmospheric Administration (NOAA) discovered the first evidence that global warming was affecting our weather — specifically a rising trend in the number of extreme weather events. The data showed more intense snowfalls, more winter precipitation, as well as more droughts, floods, and heat waves.[14] NOAA later concluded that the growing weather extremes were due to rising levels of greenhouse gases.

More recently, a team of climatologists from the NOAA found that, while the planet had been warming throughout the century, the rate of warming has tripled since 1976. Tom Karl, the leader of the team, speculated that the planet might have experienced a "change point" at which the rate of warming suddenly accelerated.[15] In other research, the NOAA found that not only was the climate getting warmer but so was the ocean.

Surprisingly, the consequences of ocean temperatures being a tad warmer are quite significant. As the ocean warms, it expands. That causes sea levels to rise, a fact that has already affected hundreds of thousands. In 2000, for example, floods kept two-thirds of Bangladesh under water for two months. Thirty of the world's largest cities are close to sea level, including London, New York, and Shanghai. If sea levels should rise more than expected because of sudden climatic changes we cannot predict, all of these cities could be at risk.

Scientists are most worried about the warming of deep-ocean currents, which travel in loops throughout the oceans and act to regulate the climate. Most of us are familiar with the Gulf Stream, which brings warm water northward along the East Coast of the United States toward Iceland. Along the way, the water exchanges heat with air, warming the air and cooling the water in the process. Water evaporates from the surface and leaves behind dissolved salt, which makes surface water denser as it moves north. Near Iceland, the surface water becomes denser than the water below it, and it sinks.

The dense, cold water then moves south along the bottom of the Atlantic, around Africa, and into the Indian Ocean, eventually mixing again with warm water and rising back to the surface. Any alterations in the path of the conveyor belt would change climate in much the same way that turning off the furnace fan changes the temperature distribution in a house. Scientists believe that historical climate changes can largely be explained by different patterns of ocean circulation.

Geological evidence suggests that the current can switch off on short notice. The trigger is an increase in fresh water from melting ice in the Arctic, which dilutes the salt water and stops it from sinking. If the current switches off, temperatures in Europe would drop so suddenly that, within ten years, London's climate in winter would resemble Siberia's.[16] One of the deep-water currents flowing south from the Greenland Sea has already stopped and gone into reverse. Upon investigation, scientists found that melting glaciers in Greenland were pouring unprecedented amounts of fresh water into the area.[17]

In a February 2002 meeting of renowned oceanographers, new data on the "North Atlantic freshening" prompted many scientists to agree that salinity levels in the North Atlantic are approaching a density very close to the critical point at which the waters will stop sinking.[18] In 2003, Terry Joyce, of the Woods Hole Oceanographic Institute, said, "I'm in the dark as to how close to an edge or transition to a new ocean and climate regime we might be. But I know which way we are walking. We are walking toward the cliff."[19]

Scientists also fear that global warming is beginning to feed on itself. One example is the tundra that is prevalent over much of Canada and Siberia. For thousands of years, the tundra has acted as a "carbon sink" by absorbing large quantities of methane and carbon dioxide. Unfortunately, since 1982, the tundra has begun to thaw. Now, rather than a helpful sink, the tundra has become a harmful source of methane and carbon dioxide. This has been occurring because the warmer climate has caused the tundra to thaw, and as it does, it releases those previously stored greenhouse gases back into the atmosphere. Methane, which traps sixty-two times more heat than carbon dioxide, accelerates global warming even further when it escapes back into the atmosphere.[20] Scientists worry that this process could trigger a rapid spurt of new warming that will feed on itself – melting more glaciers and Arctic ice, raising sea levels, and prompting heavier rainfalls in certain regions.

Early Impacts

While many see the breakup of the Antarctic ice shelf as the most dramatic manifestation of global warming, other early impacts of global warming are emerging from around the world. Lately, we have seen more intense rainfalls, severe snowstorms, hurricanes, droughts, flooding, and killer heat waves. According to an overwhelming consensus of scientific thought, all of these disasters find their genesis in global warming. Not only have disasters proliferated around the globe, climatologists expect them to increase. Of course, the number of insurance claims for weather-related disasters will also increase.

The consensus among scientists and climatologists is that, unless the world gets half of its energy from noncarbon sources by 2018, the planet will see a quadrupling of atmospheric carbon levels, which would have a catastrophic effect on climate. So far, all the early impacts that we have seen — glaciers melting, violent storms, flooding, forest fires, droughts, rising sea levels, and earlier springs — have resulted from just one degree of warming. Scientists believe that earth will warm from four to ten degrees by as early as the middle of the century. We may not have that long. Paleontological records show that prehistoric changes in carbon dioxide concentrations correlate very closely with rapid, dramatic snaps in the climate. Whether or not that happens, escaping cataclysmic climate change for several more decades is increasingly becoming a best-case scenario. A significant number of scientists now claim that it is too late to avoid major climate-related catastrophes.

Since we do not know at exactly what point the atmospheric carbon level will snap the climate — possibly because of ocean currents slowing down or stopping — we can only hope that massive mobilization to arrest global warming comes about in time. Oddly, however, while the administration publicly downplays the threat of global warming, the national security establishment is actively preparing for the kind of large-scale political destabilization it would unleash.

Anticipating the possibility of a rapid climate snap, a new Pentagon scenario envisions far more violent storms and more mega droughts in continental interiors. Pentagon planners describe masses of refugees from Mexico, South America, and the Caribbean swarming U.S. borders in search of food. In Europe, they foresee a deep freeze propelling large numbers of people from Scandinavia, Germany, and other parts of northern Europe into Spain, Italy, and points south. Intense monsoons and droughts would devastate China's food supplies. According to Pentagon planners, countries would battle over dwindling amounts of arable land, shrinking supplies of potable water, and increasingly scarce parcels of climatically hospitable territory.[21]

The Costs of Global Warming

According to the World Health Organization, 160,000 people each year die from the effects of global warming, and that number will rise into the millions in the near future from the spread of various infectious diseases, increased heat stress, and the warming-driven proliferation of allergens.[22] "There is growing evidence that changes in the global climate will have profound effects on the health and well-being of citizens in countries around the world,"[23] said Kerstin Leitner, assistant director-general of the World Health Organization.

The cost of property damage from climate change continues to rise, as does the vulnerability of insurance companies to gargantuan future claims. In the 1990s, insurance companies lost an average of $12 billion a year in property claims compared to $2 billion a year in the 1980s. In 1998 alone, they lost more than they did throughout the entire decade of the 1980s.[24]

The U.N. estimates that global warming will cause as much as $150 billion a year in damages before the end of the decade. The effect on insurance companies, of course, will be substantial. In many coastal areas of the United States, it is almost impossible to get property insurance. State Farm Insurance has stopped writing policies in Florida and many other states, claiming losses in its business because of storms and floods. Insurers could find themselves liable for damages to homes and businesses resulting from rising sea levels, storms, and floods.

Polluted Politics

Will our government save us from global warming? Let's have a look at the evidence. Big oil has done a marvelous job covering up the increasing evidence that global warming is a significant threat to the planet. Throughout the 1990s, Exxon Mobile provided funding for any "greenhouse skeptic" they could turn up and, according to the *New York Times*, gave more than $1 million a year to an array of right-wing organizations opposing action on climate change.[25]

Their efforts succeeded; not only did they manage to confuse the public, but they also confused the legislature. This is what Republican Senator James Inhofe said on the Senate floor, even as recently as July 28, 2003: ". . . Could it be that man-made global warming is the greatest hoax ever perpetuated on the American people? It sure sounds like it."[26]

The senator's remark is perplexing given that in 1995, more than two thousand of the world's top scientists unanimously concluded that global warming was, undeniably, the result of greenhouse gas emissions. This report, given to the United Nations, was the largest and most rigorously peer-reviewed scientific collaboration in history. Because of this report, 116 countries signed the Kyoto treaty, crafted to get industrial nations to cut their aggregate carbon emissions below 1990 levels by 2012. Bush refused to sign the treaty, claiming that to do so would hurt the United States economically.

As to whether the United States will rejoin the talks anytime soon, we can only judge by what the administration's chief climate negotiator, Harlan Watson, said in May 2002. In a talk in London, Watson declared that the United States would not involve itself in the Kyoto process for at least ten years. "The next time we take stock on climate change has been set by the president at 2012," he said.[27]

Mr. Watson is clearly ignorant of the fact that around 125,000 years ago, the earth was just slightly warmer than it is today. Almost overnight, half of Greenland's ice cap melted and sea levels rose approximately fifteen feet. Subsequently, the ocean current stopped and the world plunged into an ice age lasting over 100,000 years.[28]

We have now examined the first six of the seven geopolitical crises that will contribute to the perfect financial storm and promote future inflation. They are:

1. The budget deficit
2. The Social Security and Medicare crises
3. The healthcare crisis
4. The trade deficit
5. The energy crisis
6. Global warming

The next crisis is entirely man-made and only mankind can change it.

Ticking Time Bomb #7 ~ Terrorism

America has declared war on terrorism. As we know, wars are inflationary because they are expensive. To finance them, the government must either borrow money or print it. In the war against terrorism, the United States will first try to borrow money. However, as we've already discussed, it is questionable how much longer it will be able to do that. Eventually, the government will have no other choice but to print money. In order to gauge that possibility, we must examine the risks of terrorism and the costs to protect our country.

The Risks of Terrorism

A study of demographics and social trends indicates that the probabilities of future terrorism against the United States are high. The population of the Arab world is exploding, and, a great unrest exists among Arab youth, stemming largely from economic disadvantages and high unemployment.

Muslim countries continue to face serious economic problems with no improvement in sight. Traditionally, citizens of these countries have blamed their failures on foreigners rather than their own shortcomings, and it is likely that their frustrations will continue to foster the jihad against the West. Funding from international Muslim organizations has allowed terrorists to establish camps for ideological indoctrination and military training. For that reason, we can expect the number of terrorist groups throughout the world to increase in the years ahead.

Antiglobalism is the defining element that unites the many terrorist organizations. Antiglobalism means the opposition of capitalism, western corporate power, and the Americanization of the world. The terrorists believe that globalization perpetuates social injustices. They argue that global capitalism is far more concerned with expanding markets than with democracy, education, or social opportunities.

The proliferation of biological and nuclear weapons in the world poses one of the gravest threats to America. Pakistan and India have both become nuclear powers. Pakistan is an extremely lawless state where terrorism, robbery, and kidnapping are a way of life. The risk is that nuclear weapons could easily fall into the hands of terrorists if political chaos were to ensue.

Another risk, equally chilling, is that terrorist groups will someday use chemical or biological weapons. Now, state arsenals and laboratories in Pakistan are the main source of such weapons. However, these weapons could someday fall into terrorist hands because of a coup or civil war. The consequences are almost unthinkable. The U.S. government has estimated that a biological attack (Ebola, smallpox, tularemia, or anthrax) could cause one million casualties or more if released in a major American city.

The Costs of Protection

A large increase in the Homeland Security budget will be necessary to protect Americans from the threat of terrorism. Some of the areas that will require funding include:

- first responders
- healthcare system
- cargo containers
- immigration control

First responders are the country's fire, police, and emergency personnel. They remain underequipped and undertrained for the task. The estimated cost to prepare first responders for a non-nuclear attack is $62 billion over five years.

Acute-care hospitals have few quarantine or decontamination facilities and very little surge capacity in beds. Vaccines for major biological threats remain under stocked. National Guard and reserve personnel and even many professionals in our public health network have little or no training in responding to a nuclear or biological emergency. The minimal estimated cost to remedy the problem is $36 billion over five years.

Sixteen million cargo containers come into the United States each year at three hundred commercial ports of entry before being loaded onto trains and trucks. Only 2 percent are inspected. John Meredith, CEO of Hutchinson Port Holdings, one of the world's largest cargo firms, suggests that smuggling a weapon of mass destruction through containers is a question of when, not if. One recent study concludes that the current odds of detecting a shielded nuke inside a container are only about 10 percent. The minimal estimated cost to remedy the problem is $20 billion initially with ongoing yearly costs unknown.

Currently, federal agencies are unable to adequately prevent the illegal entry of aliens or locate them once they are here. There are an estimated eight to twelve million illegal aliens in the United States at this time. Few terrorism experts believe we can attain an adequate margin of safety without total overhaul of our immigration system. The minimal estimated cost is unknown but very large.

We must conclude that probabilities are very high that America will spend progressively more each year on homeland security. It is impossible to tell how much money and where the money will be spent, but we must expect the monies to come from additional borrowing or taxes. Since the end of the cold war, we have partially offset the growing costs of Social Security and Medicare by reducing military spending. Clinton was able to make somewhat optimistic projections regarding future retirement benefits by assuming that defense spending would continue to decline. That, however, is no longer the case. Defense spending is now growing faster than the economy, and there are no signs that this trend will reverse.[29]

The Costs of Empire

The modern, high-tech military machine is outrageously expensive. For much of our history, the cost of war involved fatigues, boots, K-rations, and a rifle. Now, the logistics involved in engagement are more like a NASA moon launch.

The Pentagon intends to beef up the military to the tune of about $100 billion a year. Don't expect to find that expenditure in the budget, however; no projections for future military expenditures are included. Instead, the country obtains these funds through emergency appropriations. As far as the American public is concerned, there is no difference. According to the Congressional Budget Office, new military spending over the next decade will cost $1.1 trillion (about $1,100 per year, per taxpayer), assuming no further military operations abroad over the next ten years.

To appreciate the potential for inflation caused by military expenditures, it is necessary to understand foreign policy, but foreign policy is often conducted behind closed doors for national security reasons. Two documents that most accurately depict our government's future foreign policy are the "National Security Strategy" and "Rebuilding America's Defenses: Strategy, Force and Resources for a New Century." The first document calls for a further extension of U.S. military dominance and a more aggressive approach toward countries that block u.s. interests.[30] The second document, "Rebuilding America's Defenses: Strategy, Force and Resources for a New Century," is essentially a blueprint for an American military and foreign policy goal to end any potentially meaningful military opposition to u.s. power. To support that goal, it calls for increased military spending and a dramatic transformation of both military technology and the role of the military.[31]

As if anticipating that U.S. foreign policy would encounter resistance, military planners are already thinking ahead. They believe that the control of space is critical and that we must monopolize this domain of warfare and be ready to control disorder by using space systems for precision strikes from space to counter the possibility of the use of weapons of mass destruction. The "Star Wars" program, first inaugurated in 1983, has now cost $70 billion. The Congressional Budget Office estimates that current plans to augment that program will cost an additional $60 billion, while some private estimates are much higher.

A global arms race is now underway as countries prepare to fight for the world's remaining natural resources, essential to the functioning of modern societies.

As America rearms, other nations emulate our lead. In response to u.s. plans for nuclear escalation, China, Russia, and India are rushing head-long to develop their own arsenals. Analysts have estimated that Russian military expenditures have tripled since Bush took office. Putin cited the Bush doctrine of preemptive strike, and added that, like the United States, Russia would also use military force if there were an attempt to limit Russia's access to regions that are essential to its survival.[32]

To summarize, the economy of the United States is highly vulnerable to a shock resulting from any number of biological or nuclear attacks. These attacks could emanate from direct attacks by other countries or could as easily occur by accident. Even more likely is the possibility that terrorist organizations will someday obtain weapons of mass destruction and use them against us.

We can predict that the United States will spend hundreds of billions of dollars on military technology, missile defense systems, expanded bases, additional military personnel, and a series of planned engagements over a period of many years. In part 2 of this book, you will learn how to invest in specific companies and sectors that will benefit from America's rearmament as well as the inflation to which it contributes.

We have now examined all seven of the geopolitical crises that will contribute to the perfect financial storm and promote future inflation. They are:

1. The budget crisis
2. The Social Security and Medicare crises
3. The healthcare crisis
4. The trade deficit
5. The energy crisis
6. Global warming
7. Terrorism

This chapter should convince you that it is only a matter of time before we experience more inflation in this country. If you simply maintain your current investment posture, your money will continue to shrink and maintaining your current lifestyle may not be possible. Old school financial planning will fail you because it is out of touch with the new inflation paradigm. We will discuss why most people never make money in the stock market and that mutual fund investors face grave risks over the coming decade.

However, by understanding the new inflation paradigm and making selective investments that will benefit from inflation, you could make returns in just a few short years equivalent to returns over a lifetime of investing during ordinary economic times. This book will teach you how by showing you dozens of ways to profit from inflation so that you can choose the types of investments that fit your own level of expertise and risk tolerance.

No investment book would be complete without real estate. Over the long term, real estate has always been the best hedge against inflation. My gut tells me that will continue to be the case. However, as with any asset class whose returns have run far ahead of the norm, setbacks are likely. Therefore, I will show you not only how to invest profitably in real estate but also how to protect yourself and even profit if real estate prices turn down.

Remember that reading this book is only your starting point. You will need to monitor each of the seven geopolitical crises as well as stay abreast of the best ways to profit from them. For example, several new exchange-traded funds (ETFs) and mutual funds geared toward inflation are in the planning stages. Look for useful updates to this book at www.HoneyWhoShrunkOurMoney.com. With that, I invite you to turn the page and start thinking like a capitalist.

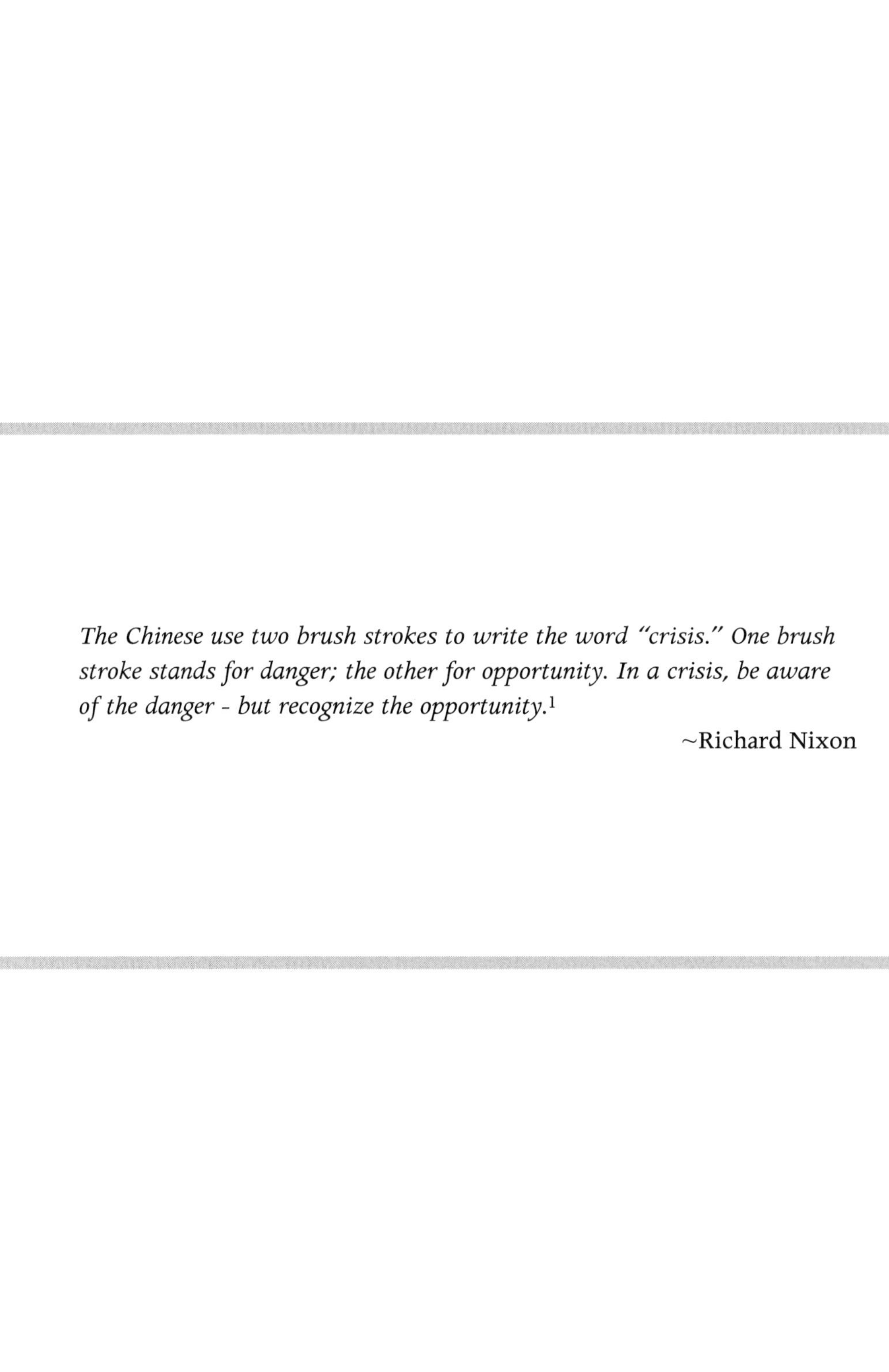

The Chinese use two brush strokes to write the word "crisis." One brush stroke stands for danger; the other for opportunity. In a crisis, be aware of the danger - but recognize the opportunity.[1]

~Richard Nixon

How to Protect Your Savings and Profit from America's Woes

How to Protect Yourself on Wall Street

Wealth is an application of mind to nature; and the art of getting rich consists not so much in industry, much less in saving, but in a better order, in timeliness, in being at the right spot.[1]

~ Ralph Waldo Emerson,

In the previous chapter, you learned the answer to the question posed by the book's title — who shrunk our money? Place the blame at the feet of the Federal Reserve who have continually diluted the value of your dollars by adding more of them and the politicians who borrowed and spent money they did not have. In this chapter, you will learn about stock market myths and how to protect yourself on Wall Street.

Pick up nearly any magazine on personal finance, have a chat with your financial representative, or turn on CNBC. In three-part harmony, this chorus will always sing the same refrain: buy good quality stocks for the long haul or invest in mutual funds. How good is that advice? To answer that question, we need to take a hard look at what the financial community has led us to believe about the stock market.

The Myth of the Institution

One of the most pervasive myths in our society is that the stock market is an institution that offers the average investor a way to increase his wealth. The idea is that by owning shares in some of the country's largest and most profitable companies, the investor will receive dividends (a portion of the company's profits) and participate in the company's growth. As the company grows, it will produce more earnings. Higher earnings will cause the price of the stock to go up. The basic idea makes a lot of sense.

The truth of the stock market is quite different. Market insiders make most of the money made in the stock market. Market insiders are corporate executives, brokerage firms, and stock market exchanges. Let's see how these three businesses work together.

If the stock market did not exist, companies would not be able to grow as quickly as they do. Whenever they wanted to expand, they would need to borrow money from banks. However, because of the stock market and the help of brokerage firms, corporations can raise tens of millions of dollars without having to pay anything for the money. They simply print up pieces of paper (shares) that state whoever owns the shares owns a miniscule portion of the company. The process of getting the public to hand over millions of dollars to them is called an underwriting. The underwriting is a beautiful thing for all parties involved – everyone gets rich overnight.

Often, those investors who get in early on an initial public offering (IPO) make out well, as small investors who would like to own shares in the company — but were not lucky enough to get shares during the IPO — bid up the stock price once it begins to trade on the open market. Regardless of what happens to the price of the stock or the company, for that matter, both the company and the underwriter walk away with millions of dollars. Quite frankly, the stock market is not a risky place for insiders.

The stock market's only purpose is to transfer wealth and risk capital from the public to corporations. As part of the process, corporations, brokerage firms, and stock market exchanges make money. The corporation gets free money from the underwriting. The brokerage firm that performed the underwriting gets a huge fee and a sizable number of shares of stock. As soon as the shares start selling, they will make commissions. The exchanges collect a small fee every time someone buys or sell shares of the stock.

Because the brokerage firm that brought the company public retains a large number of shares as part of the underwriting, it is in their best interest to see the stock price go higher. This is where the fun begins. To get the stock price higher, they must promote the stock.

In the old days, it worked like this: the firm employed both stockbrokers and analysts. It was the stockbroker's job to promote stocks to clients and encourage them to make trades, thus increasing transaction volume for the firm. However, it was the analyst's job to research a company's prospects for profitability and write research reports. A good research department could supposedly find superior companies, which the broker could then advise his customers to buy. If the stock went up, the customers were happy and they would buy again the next time the broker called.

These days, however, analysts' opinions can no longer be trusted. Analysts have a conflict of interest with the companies for which their brokerage firms provide underwriting services. Now, analysts notoriously write favorable research reports to promote companies that their firm underwrote.

Moreover, these days, most analysts are perpetually bullish on nearly all stocks. Practically every stock receives a rating of "Buy" or "Strong Buy." Sometimes — if a company's prospects seem uncommonly abysmal — an analyst might reduce his rating to an "Accumulate" or a "Hold," but never a "Sell." One example of unbridled, yet unfounded, analyst optimism occurred during the latter part of the 1990s. If you traded stocks at that time, you are probably familiar with the names Mary Meeker and Henry Blodgett. These two Internet analysts achieved celebrity status (and respective paychecks of $15 million and $25 million a year) for touting speculative stocks.

Mary Meeker worked for Morgan Stanley Dean Witter and Henry Blodgett worked for Merrill Lynch. In the old days (pre-Internet), analysts studied a company's sales, profit margins, and earnings. However, since most Internet companies had no earnings, these two analysts disregarded financial statistics and began to value companies based on "page views" and "eyeballs." In 1997, Meeker wrote,

"We have one general response to the word 'valuation' these days: Bull market . . . we believe we have entered a new valuation zone."[2]

Meeker was a perpetual bull, always reassuring clients that any setback was temporary. Even after the bubble burst and her recommended stocks were circling the drain, Meeker refused to face the music. Instead of advising clients to get out while they still could, Meeker stood by and watched her clients lose as much as 90 percent of their money.

Meeker was later criticized that her unbridled public optimism was because most of the companies she followed used Morgan Stanley Dean Witter as their investment-banking firm. While Meeker was high profile, her story is common. Stock market analysts' recommendations and forecasts in general cannot be trusted. In fact, savvy investors have learned not to listen to a word they say.

Another example of how analysts uniformly lead their clients over the proverbially cliff was the recommendations for JDS Uniphase, a popular fiber optics stock in the 1990s. Analysts from all the major firms followed JDSU. Table 3.1 provides a sampling of how they reacted as the stock tumbled.

As you can see, all the analysts' recommendations were worthless. If you had taken any of these recommendations, you would have lost as much as 98 percent of your money.[3]

One of my favorite financial writers is Alan Abelson, an editor at *Barron's* for over four decades. In writing about the qualifications for being a Wall Street analyst, he said the following:

> *You should be equipped with the kind of face that doesn't scare small children when you make your obligatory appearances on Tout TV . . . Knowing the difference between a bond and a stock is helpful but not essential. The only true requisite is that, in good times and bad, come rain or shine, whether the market is woefully depressed or really flying, you must be bullish. And that means all day, every day, including weekends, lest you lose the habit.*[4]

Table 3.1 — Analyst Recommendations for JDSU

W. R. Hambrect	First Union	Raymond James	ABN AMRO
BUY When the price was $130.87	STRONG BUY When the price was $129.06	STRONG BUY When the price was $121.37	BUY When the price was $110.37
STRONG BUY After falling to $28.53	MARKET PERFORM After falling to $38.01	MARKET PERFORM After falling to $20.82	ADD After falling to $26.94

The Myth of Corporate Responsibility

As I indicated earlier, only the public's money is at risk in the stock market. Regardless of what happens to a stock's price, the brokerage firms and the executives at the company always make out like bandits. For example, take the case of JDS Uniphase. In the year 2000, while the company bankrupted many individual investors, the CEO's total compensation was over $100 million. Meanwhile, the chairman of the board made $150 million by exercising his stock options and unloading 1.6 million shares of stock. According to the Canadian publication, *Canadian Business*, he "treated JDS Uniphase shares like hot potatoes – the second he got them, usually through exercising options, he's on the phone to his broker screaming sell, sell, sell."[5]

Global Crossing is another company that made its executives rich, while common stockholders were massacred. The CEO, Gary Winnick, walked away with over $700 million from converting his free stock options to stock, which he sold while the public was buying. With the money, he was able to purchase one of the most expensive homes in America, the Hilton estate in Bel Air, California, which he purchased for $40 million.[6] Meanwhile, investors in his company lost everything. In January 2002, the company went bankrupt, but Winnick still lives in a $40 million mansion.

In 1999, Charles Wang, CEO of Computer Associates, was the highest paid CEO in the country, earning $507 million dollars. In the years 1998,

1999, and 2000 combined, his total compensation was $698.2 million. Was he worth that kind of money? *Business Week* quoted the company's spokespersons as saying that he was "worth every penny of his pay."[7] His shareholders, who lost 63 percent of their investment during the same period, might disagree.

A few years earlier, in 1995, Michael Eisner was the highest paid CEO in America, commanding a cool $194 million salary. During the same three-year period that Wang brought in $698.2 million, Eisner took home $699.1 million at Disney. Net income for his company fell by more than half during that period and the stock dropped 10 percent. You might wonder why the board of directors, who sets the compensation for executives, would pay him such an exorbitant amount while the company's net income was declining. Further investigation would provide an answer. It seems that Eisner handpicked his own board of directors, a common practice in corporate America. Among others, the Disney board boasted the principal of his child's elementary school, Sidney Poitier, the architect who designed his home, and a university president whose school got a $1 million donation from Eisner.[8]

Fortune Magazine looked at all major companies whose stock had declined by more than 75 percent from 1999 to 2002, and found that, on average, executives walked away with $50 million each. Phil Anschutz, of Quest Communications, took the prize with $1.5 billion. During the same time that he was raking in the money, his company's stock fell from $50 to $5 per share.[9]

The Art of Skimming

Corporate CEOs skim the cream off the top regardless of how well they run the company. In 2000, the average CEO of a major corporation earned $20 million. The twenty highest paid CEOs averaged $117.6 million each. The pay for CEOs in the 1990s increased 571 percent, while corporate profits only increased 114 percent.[10] Imagine if your pay went up five times faster than the profits of your company. Wouldn't it seem as though something was askew?

Look at the year 2000. The S&P was down 10 percent, the NASDAQ was down 39 percent, salaried workers averaged a 4 percent increase, but

CEO salaries increased 22 percent with an additional 50 percent increase in stock option compensation.[11]

These stock options that CEOs and other executives are awarded dilute the value of the stock for all investors when the options are converted to stock and then sold. If the stock goes down before the insiders get a chance to sell, the board can issue more options at a lower price, even below the market price of the stock. Both ways, they win and you lose.

Moreover, the very nature of employee stock options can tempt management to manipulate earnings to prop up the stock price long enough to exercise their options and dump their shares. Such tactics can hurt the long-term prospects of the company and affect the investors who bought the stock as a long-term investment, often in their IRA.

These examples should convince you that the stock market is a rigged game designed for the benefit of corporations, brokerage firms, and exchanges. Here's the game in the nutshell:

- Brokerage firms make huge fees through underwritings. Next, they promote the stock to their customers to drive the stock price up. Finally, after inflating the stock price, they sell their shares that they had received at the underwriting.
- Analysts write biased research reports, which their brokers use as sales tools to get customers to buy stocks.
- Corporations get free money through underwritings, a portion of which goes directly to the owners. CEOs and top executives set themselves up with exorbitant salaries and stock options, which further dilute the value of the stock.
- Managements frequently use aggressive accounting techniques to manipulate financial statements to make the company look good in the near-term, while long-term investors pay the price. A case in point is AOL, one of the favorite stocks of the 1990s.

The Myth of Financial Transparency

Nearly all investors owned AOL in the late 1990s. Along with stocks like Intel and Cisco, investment advisors touted AOL as the kind of stock you would want to own for the long run. I owned AOL in my IRA, and my children owned AOL in their college funds. It was a great stock for kids because they could easily relate to its business.

AOL dominated its industry; no other company even came close to its market share, nor, it seemed, ever would. Furthermore, AOL had the whole world to conquer, so it appeared that its business was still in its infancy. What really set AOL apart, however, was the fact that — unlike almost all other Internet companies — AOL had earnings, or so we thought.

AOL's marketing strategy was both bold and ingenious. They sent free software to everyone in the country. The strategy appeared to work; each month thousands of people signed up for the AOL service. What investors did not realize, however, was that the huge expenses of these marketing campaigns were not showing up on their financial statements. By some accounting magic, or trickery, the marketing expenses were deferred into the future. If the accounting had been done properly, AOL would have showed losses instead of profits and the stock price would have commanded a far lower premium.

Using only its stock, AOL acquired Time Warner in January of 2000. AOL's stock price, of course, was inflated because of fraudulent accounting. Five months later, the SEC uncovered the improper accounting and fined AOL $3.5 million. By then, AOL had already acquired one of the largest news organizations in the world, and AOL's top executives had walked away with $3 billion.

After the merger, the new stock dropped like a stone. Within three years, the market value of the new company had fallen from $334 billion to $60 billion.[12]

The Myth of the Long Haul

The story of AOL should make you stop and think before buying an individual stock. Ask yourself the following questions:

- What do I really know about this company?
- How could unexpected geopolitical events affect its future earnings?
- What competitor could take its market share?
- How is its debt structured and how would a change in interest rates affect its net profit?

- Who is selling me the stock that I am buying, and why is he selling?
- Am I paying too much for the stock?
- How do I know that the financials are accurate?
- How could I really know that I was not buying another Enron?

If you are honest with yourself, I think you will agree that you have no way of knowing everything you need to know to make an intelligent investment. In truth, you are making a huge leap of faith and taking a gamble.

In addition to the fact that we can no longer trust a company's financials, the lesson to learn from AOL is that buying any stock for the long haul is not a good idea. There have always been darlings, — Xerox, IBM, and GM to name a few. However, because of unanticipated competition or technological change, these stocks lost their luster. If we should avoid investing in individual stocks for the long haul, should we invest in a diversified portfolio instead?

The mutual fund industry would like you to believe that. Unfortunately, that is a myth also. It is easy to show someone a chart of the Dow Jones Industrial Average dating back to the early 1900s and convince him that, with the exception of an occasional crash and intermittent bear markets, the market has marched inexorably higher. There are two objections I have to that argument. The first is that long-term charts of the stock market do not consider the effect of inflation. In fact, since the early 1900s, the dollar has lost 98 percent of its value. What good is it to own stocks for twenty or thirty years if inflation erodes the bulk of their gains?

The second argument is that, whether a long-term hold succeeds or not is highly dependent on timing and a great deal of luck. For example, if you had invested in the stock market at any time during the thirty-year period from 1899 to 1929, you would have lost money by 1932. The stock market crash wiped out thirty-three years of market gains.

If you were late getting in the 1920s bull market, you would not have shown a profit until 1954. The market took twenty-five years to recover to its post-crash peak. Therefore, we can conclude that, unless your timing was good and you were extremely lucky, the first half of the century would not have delivered great investment returns to the buy-and-hold investor.

The 1950s and 1960s offered a more benign investment climate because our economy was growing and interest rates were low. However, a bear market occurred in the late 1960s, followed by a much deeper bear market in 1973 1974, which nearly cut the S&P 500 in half. Had you invested in 1961, you would have lost all your gains by 1974. Had you invested in September 1968, you would not have made money for the next ten years. Meanwhile, inflation would have continued to erode the value of your dollars.

The crash beginning in 2000 erased 72 percent of the NASDAQ. A $100,000 portfolio in March of 2000 would have been worth only $28,000 by September of 2001. The market would need to rise 256 percent from its low to return the investor his $100,000. At 12 percent per year, that would take close to twenty years. Meanwhile, inflation would have eroded the value of your dollars. The simple fact is that successful long-term investing is highly dependent on impeccable timing; without a great deal of luck, your odds are not good.

The Myth of Professional Management

The majority of the public invests in the stock market through mutual funds. Additionally, there are more mutual funds than there are stocks listed on the New York Stock Exchange. One of the reasons that mutual funds play such a dominant role in the stock market is because most people participate in the stock market primarily through their 401(k) plans, which limit investment options primarily to stock funds, bond funds, and money market funds.

Other people also invest their IRAs and other savings in mutual funds, hoping to benefit from professional management, which should provide the investor an edge over simply buying a market index. Let's see if it does.

Dr. Burton G. Malkiel in his 1985 book, *A Random Walk Down Wall Street* concluded that it was difficult, if not impossible, for the average active professional money manager to consistently beat an index of stocks. He says, "A blindfolded monkey throwing darts could theoretically pick stocks as well as a professional."[13] Thus, investors would be better off buying an unmanaged index of stocks instead of using a professional or trying to manage the funds themselves.

Studies that are more recent have corroborated Malkiel's research.

In his 1997 book *Winning the Losers Game*, Charles Ellis analyzed a twenty-five-year period and reported that 75 percent of professionally managed funds underperformed the S&P 500.[14]

Also in 1997, Ira Weiss, an accounting professor at Columbia Business School, went back thirty-six years and found that diversified funds gained an average of 12 percent per year less than the S&P 500 index.[15]

Finally, another analysis, cited by Max Isaacman, author of *How to Be an Index Investor*, indicated that 96 percent of professional money managers underperformed the S&P 500 index.[16]

If investors believe they are going to be able to pick the best manager among the bunch, their logic is likely to backfire on them. Because managers have different styles and prefer different types of investments, the cyclic nature of the market dictates that this year's best manager is likely to be next year's worst. The same reasoning holds true, not just for a year, but also for any period that you are likely to select.

In selecting a fund, you are selecting a manager, but managers change jobs frequently. Managers who have had success running a particular fund often leave to accept a better offer or to start their own fund. Thus, the most popular funds of today can be the dogs of tomorrow. For example, for years, the Janus family of funds was a top choice among no-load funds. However, in a little more than three years between March 2000 and May 2002, the Janus Fund lost 46 percent, Janus Twenty lost 61 percent, and Janus Worldwide lost 49 percent.[17]

We have now examined the results of numerous studies, which proved that mutual funds consistently underperform the overall market. In fact, that is common knowledge. What is less well known is that the average investor in mutual funds does even worse. The evidence comes from the Boston based research firm Dalbar Incorporated.

In 2001, they conducted a study that examined investor returns from January 1994 through December 2000, a very bullish market period. While the S&P averaged a gain of 16.3 percent per year, the individual equity mutual fund investor only realized an annual return of 5.32 percent per year. Further investigation found that mutual fund investments were held for an average of 2.6 years.[18] The evidence indicates that investors underperformed the overall market by a wide margin simply because they chased after the best performing funds.

In another study, which sought to determine how investors' returns compared to those of mutual funds, Professor Charles Trzcinka of Indiana University examined 6,900 mutual funds from 1998 to 2001. On average, investors underperformed the funds they were invested in by 82 percent. In one example, the study showed that the Fidelity Aggressive Growth fund returned 2.8 percent during the period, but the average investor in the fund lost 24.1 percent. How could that happen? Again, the only explanation is that investors attempted to time the market, switching funds at the most inopportune times. According to the professor,

"The sheer magnitude of the difference we discovered between the total returns earned by mutual funds and the results captured by the average shareholder is shocking and tragic."[19]

The brokerage industry, of course, is aware of this. However, they are not about to tell you. Instead, they would prefer to tantalize you with charts of market index returns, knowing that, in fact, the average investor never comes close to those returns.

Meanwhile, the mutual fund industry advertises the returns of leading funds, knowing full well that investors will not achieve such returns because today's leaders will be tomorrow's laggards. As the average investor chases after the leaders, he will continually find himself getting in late. Over time, he will be disappointed with his selection, rethink his decision, and switch to another fund.

The Myth of the "Averages"

The brokerage industry likes to display very long-term charts of market averages to prove that the market always goes up over time. For example, a chart of the entire twentieth century would show most major averages growing by an average of about 6.7 percent per year. However, stock market averages are not truthful representations of what an investor is likely to make in the stock market. Here's why.

1. *Like a professional football team, the composition of market averages change over time.*

   Over time, companies go out of business, shrink in size, or otherwise falter and are dropped from the averages. Companies that stumble are replaced with new, growing companies, like Wal-Mart and Microsoft. For example, the s&p 500 index today is not composed of the same companies that were in it twenty-five years ago. If you had invested in all 500 companies in the s&p 500 twenty-five years ago and still owned those stocks, you would own some bankrupt companies and you would not own Wal-Mart and Microsoft. Your return would not resemble the return of the s&p 500 for the last twenty-five years. My guess is that your broker did not take the time to explain that to you.

2. *Stock market averages do not account for the fact that investors must pay commissions and must buy at the ask price and sell at the bid price.*

   An index assumes no trading. But in the real world you pay commissions and have slippage costs. Slippage occurs because you must always buy the stock at the asking price and sell the stock at the bid. Therefore, you will always pay more than the market price when you buy and you will always receive less than the market price when you sell.

3. *Investors typically act on limited information, often buying stocks on the advice of others.*

   The *Hulbert Financial Digest* is the leading authority on stock market newsletter advisors. In a recent eleven-year study, it found that the average newsletter's model portfolio did only half as well as the Wilshire 5000 index. Furthermore, only six out of fifty-five advisers followed managed to beat the market; in other words, 87 percent of professional advisers, who make their living attempting to find superior stocks and funds, could not beat the market.

4. *An investor is not likely to make a multidecade investment.*
   Investors put money in the market when they have it (for example, after receiving an inheritance) and take it out when they need it (to pay for college, weddings, home improvements, and so forth). According to Dalbar Inc.'s study, even mutual fund investors' average holding period was only 2.4 years. Moreover, investors often attempt market timing, leaving the market during bear markets and re-entering in bull markets. Finally, even when they're in the market, investors will often change funds or stocks, generally at the wrong times.

5. *Mutual funds underperform market averages and mutual fund investors underperform mutual funds.*
   Research studies have shown that, even during bull markets, mutual funds have only done one-third as well as the S&P 500. Moreover, other studies have shown that investors do only one-fifth as well as the funds in which they invest.

In summary, we can see that most investors do not make money in the stock market for a number of reasons. However, even investors who have been disciplined enough to invest long term and fortunate enough to have invested in reasonably good funds have found themselves sitting ducks for market crashes and intermittent bear markets.

Once an investor has been unlucky enough to experience a sharp setback to his portfolio, he is unlikely to recover for many years. The most recent bear market was one such example. According to an Economic Policy Institute briefing paper titled "Retirement out of Reach," it will take the average household over thirty years to recover the wealth lost in 2000 and 2001 from market declines.[20]

The Myth of Conservative Investing

Psychographics is the study of the psychological profiles of buyers. Regarding the world of investments, we know that younger investors are more active, while older investors are more passive. Younger investors also take more risks, while older investors are more risk adverse.

Risk-adverse investors, caught off guard, will suffer the most in the years ahead. Those in their forties and fifties, buffeted by a series of financial shocks, will see hopes for early retirement vanish before their eyes. They will struggle to maintain their income as weak corporate profits force their employers to keep a lid on wage increases in order to maintain profitability. Meanwhile, their savings, most likely invested in stocks and bonds through 401(k) plans, will quite possibly decline. All the while, they will face even larger fixed expenses as their children enter college and their parents enter nursing homes.

For as long as I can remember, the brokerage and financial planning industries have advised their clients to reduce their stock holdings and increase their bond holdings as they got older. The theory is that a sixty-five-year-old will have less time to recover from a severe bear market in stocks. However, I have never seen the financial industry warn investors about a severe bear market in bonds. In my opinion, they should.

The value of bonds that you own is inversely related to current long-term interest rates. As interest rates rise, the bonds you own are worth less; as interest rates fall, they are worth more. In the case of rising rates, the bonds already issued (the ones that you own) must be priced lower in order to yield as much as new bonds that are issued at a higher rate of interest.

Bond investments may be for ten, twenty, or even thirty years. The longer the average maturity of your portfolio, the greater the price change will be as interest rates rise. Furthermore, the lower that overall interest rates are, the greater the impact will be on prices once interest rates start moving higher. For example, when interest rates are at 4 percent, a one-point increase to five percent represents a 25 percent change in yield.

Imagine the severe effect on your portfolio if you had bonds yielding only 4 percent, and interest rates went to 8 or even 12 percent. You could easily see the value of your portfolio cut in half. Additionally, higher interest rates would mean higher inflation. Therefore, the fixed interest payments that you receive from your bonds would buy even less than before.

Now You Know Better

Here is a recap of the seven stock market myths and their corresponding truths.

1. *The Myth of the Institution:* The stock market offers the average investor superior returns.
   Truth: The stock market is a rigged game, designed to benefit corporations, stock market exchanges, and brokerage firms.

2. *The Myth of Corporate Responsibility:* Corporate executives act in the best interest of their shareholders.
   Truth: Corporate executives act in their own best interest.

3. *The Myth of Financial Transparency:* Investors can judge a company's profitability by examining its financial statements.
   Truth: Investors can be easily misled by financial subterfuge.

4. *The Myth of the Long Haul:* Investing for the long haul makes good financial sense.
   Truth: Depending on when you invest, it can take thirty years to get your money back.

5. *The Myth of Professional Management:* The professional management offered by mutual funds benefits the investor.
   Truth: Nearly all mutual fund managers underperform the market.

6. *The Myth of the Averages:* Stock market averages show that stock prices rise over time.
   Truth: Stock market averages change composition over time as companies that underperform or go bankrupt are jettisoned. Additionally, stock market averages do not account for commission costs and slippage.

7. *The Myth of Conservative Investing:* Investing in a balanced portfolio of stocks and bonds insulates the investor from market downturns. *Truth:* During periods of rising long-term interest rates, the value of both stocks and bonds decline.

In summary, the stock market is not what it appears to be. Like a Las Vegas casino, the stock market exists for one reason: to separate you from your money. Brokerage firms, mutual funds, and financial planners — all who benefit from getting you to play the game — bombard you with propaganda to obscure the truth. Now you know better.

However, while most approaches to stock market investing fail, you are going to learn how to invest selectively in specific companies and ETFs (exchange-traded funds) that are positioned to benefit from the coming inflation. To maximize your gains, however, you need to know how to keep your profits from shrinking because of taxes. In the next chapter, you will learn the five best ways to do that.

4

How to Protect Your Profits When You Make Them

The avoidance of taxes is the only intellectual pursuit that carries any reward.[1]

~ John Maynard Keynes

Before you start making investments based on what you learn in this book, you need to know how to protect the money you will make from your investments. In this chapter, you will learn not one, not two, but five ways to do that. When you realize how much money these techniques can save you, you're going to kick yourself for not taking advantage of these gifts earlier.

How to Make a 35 Percent Return This Week

Defined pension plans have nearly gone by the wayside for most employees, now replaced by 401(k) programs. You can place a portion of your income into your 401(k). Your employer determines the exact percentage. The money that you contribute, which the government would normally tax before you receive it, goes into an account untaxed. To appreciate the benefit, assume first that you are in a 26 percent tax bracket, and second, that you are about to receive $100 from your employer in wages. The taxman steps between the two of you and snatches $26, leaving you with only $74. You would like to invest the $74. What return will you need to get back to $100? The answer is 35 percent. Therefore, if you allow your employer to put the $100 in your 401(k) instead of giving it to you, you will immediately make a 35 percent return on your investment.

Furthermore, many employers will match part or all of your contributions with their own money. If your employer were to match your contributions one for one, you would now have $200 in your 401(k) as opposed to $74 in your pocket. If you have a 401(k) plan available, contributing to it is a no-brainer. Besides making money immediately, your investments grow tax-deferred until you take them out. Here are the technical details.

Just like an IRA, you are allowed to withdraw your money from a 401(k) at age fifty-nine and one-half. You may, if you wish, leave your money there until age seventy and one-half, when you must begin withdrawing a set amount each year based on your life expectancy as defined by the IRS. If you are still working, you can keep your money in your 401(k) until you retire. Remember, money in your 401(k) is tax deferred. Once you withdraw it, you will need to pay income taxes on the entire amount. If you leave your job prior to retirement, you may transfer your assets into a new 401(k) at your new place of employment. Alternatively, if your new employer does not offer a plan, you can transfer your assets into a rollover IRA.

One problem with 401(k) plans is their limited number of investment offerings. During the eighteen-year bull market that spanned most of the 1980s and 1990s, that was a minor inconvenience. It was easy to find an assortment of good stock funds, bond funds, and balanced funds. However, if we face a decade of sub-par gains in stock and bond markets, what will you do?

My advice is that, if you leave your current employer for any reason, transfer your assets to a rollover IRA and leave them there, even if your new employer offers a 401(k) plan. You can still own an IRA even if you start a new 401(k). At least by keeping your old 401(k) money in an IRA, you will have an almost unlimited number of investment choices.

Tax Deferred Growth

IRAs come in two flavors — traditional IRAs and Roth IRAs. There is a world of difference between the two. We will first explore the traditional IRA. As long as you have earned income, the IRS allows you to contribute $4,000 per year to your IRA. Like with the 401(k), the $4,000 is exempt from income tax. Beginning in 2008, the IRS will raise the contribution level to $5,000. Your money grows tax-deferred until you are allowed to withdraw it at age 59 and one-half. If you withdraw it before then, you face paying income tax on the entire amount plus a 10 percent early withdrawal penalty.

The primary advantage of an IRA over a 401(k) is a much wider range of investment choices. You can open an account at any qualified institution, such as a bank, brokerage firm, or insurance company, and then invest in or trade a wide range of investment products. While it is common to think of an IRA as a safe place for retirement funds and long-term investments, an often-overlooked advantage is that you can use your IRA for short-term trading, while completely deferring all short-term capital gains.

Many people mistakenly believe that, because they have a 401(k), they are not eligible to contribute to a traditional IRA. That is simply not true. You can still have a separate IRA and contribute up to the maximum allowed amount. The difference is, unlike a self-employed person, who only has an IRA, your contributions will probably not be deductible. (The IRS bases the actual threshold for deductibility on your adjusted gross income and marital status.) Even without the benefit of deductions for your contributions, however, contributing to an IRA in addition to a 401(k) is a good idea if you can afford it. The reason is that all your contributions can go to work for you tax-deferred. An even better idea, however, is a Roth IRA.

Tax-Free Growth

The government created the Roth IRA as part of the Taxpayer Relief Act of 1997. While the Roth offers advantages over the traditional IRA, one distinct disadvantage is that contributions are not deductible. However, that is a small price to pay for the Roth's primary advantage, which is that your money compounds tax-free. Remember, the traditional IRA offers tax-deferred growth, not tax-free growth. The following example illustrates the difference.

Fred, who plans to retire next year at sixty, has accumulated $200,000 in his traditional IRA. His dream has been to buy a sailboat and spend the next several years island hopping in the Caribbean. If he takes the entire amount out of his IRA, he will pay approximately $53,000 in income taxes, leaving him with only $147,000 to buy a boat. If Fred had contributed to a Roth IRA instead, he could take his entire $200,000 out and pay no taxes. To achieve tax-free status, the only requirement is that you must have had your Roth for a minimum of five years. Another significant advantage of the Roth is that, unlike the traditional IRA, there is no requirement that you withdraw the funds at age 70 and one-half. Therefore, if Fred was able to buy his sailboat using another source of funds, he could keep his Roth as long as he liked.

The Roth IRA, however, does impose some eligibility restrictions that you should consider. If you are married and file separately, you cannot contribute to a Roth IRA. If you file jointly and your adjusted gross income exceeds $160,000, you are also out of luck. If you are single, the threshold is $95,000.

If you meet the eligibility criteria, I would recommend the Roth over the traditional IRA. If you already have a traditional IRA, you can convert it to a Roth without a penalty, but you must pay ordinary income tax on the proceeds from your IRA. If your adjusted income for the year is less than $100,000 and you have the additional cash to pay the tax, it may be advantageous to do so. Consult your tax advisor regarding your own situation.

There is no law against owning both a traditional IRA and a Roth IRA. In fact, you can contribute to both. For example, you could contribute $2,000 to the traditional IRA for some immediate tax benefits and $2,000 to a Roth IRA for its long-term benefits. If you are over fifty, the IRS allows you to contribute a higher than normal amount to either type of IRA. In both 2006 and 2007, you can contribute $5,000, and in 2008 and beyond you can contribute $6,000. One final tip: the difference between making your annual contribution at the first of the year as opposed to the end of the year makes a big difference over time because of the additional time that your money has to compound, so make your contribution early in the year.

The Most Flexible Shelter

The self-directed IRA, which may be either a traditional or Roth IRA, is the most flexible of all the IRAs because it expands your investment options. The company where you open your IRA is called the custodian. If you open an IRA at a bank, you will be limited in your investments to products that the bank sells. If you open an IRA at a brokerage firm, you will be limited to products offered at that brokerage firm. When you set up your account with a self-directed custodian, you will be able to take advantage of all the investments allowed by law — including those offered at banks or brokerage firms with which your custodian has relationships. In addition — and the reason that most people set up self-directed IRAs — you will be able to invest in real estate, both real property and notes.

If your IRA is small, buying a house with your IRA is impractical because, as we will see later, financing would be difficult to obtain. However, buying a vacant lot is an excellent way to invest your self-directed IRA money. You may wish to buy a lot in a new subdivision. Once all the other lots have been sold and houses have been built, your lot will most likely be worth a lot more than you paid for it. In some developments, you are required to build a house within a year or two of purchasing a lot so be sure to investigate that provision before buying. If you live in an area that is growing, it is not hard to find lots on the outskirts of town that lie in the path of future development. If you live in an area where real estate prices are stagnant, take a vacation to any of the fast-growing Sunbelt areas and make your investment there. If you have limited funds in your IRA and buying a vacant lot seems beyond your reach, don't despair. You may be able to arrange financing. Here's how it works.

The IRS will allow you to borrow money when investing your IRA only if the loan is nonrecourse. That means that the lender's only recourse, if you do not make your payments, is to take the property. Banks will not usually loan you money unless they can take recourse on you personally. However, you may be able to find a lot that the owner is willing to finance with a nonrecourse loan. If you do not make the payments, he can take the lot. If you make this kind of arrangement, make certain that you have enough money in your IRA to make the payments and pay your taxes.

What if you find a lot that you would like to buy, but the owner will not offer financing? Do you have any other options? Absolutely. First, try to find a friend or family member who would like to invest with you. Then, form a tenancy-in-common and purchase the property together. You will share proportional ownership to the degree of your contributions. Your partner can use non-IRA money for his investment, and once a tenancy-in-common has been formed, you can invest non-IRA money as well. Therefore, no property is out of reach if you can find other partners who can invest cash.

A second creative way to make this work is to form an LLC (limited liability company). An LLC is a corporation, limiting liability to each member's personal investment. However, for tax purposes, it resembles a partnership in that earnings flow through to the individual members. You can buy shares in the LLC just as you would buy shares in Microsoft. Therefore, your IRA can buy shares in the LLC. There is no limit to how many shares you can buy with your non-IRA money or the money (both IRA and non-IRA) of friends and family.

To recap, three ways to stretch your self-directed IRA are to:

- Buy property financed with a nonrecourse loan.
- Form a tenancy-in-common.
- Form an LLC.

Once you have a self-directed IRA, you can invest in mutual funds, CDs, stocks and bonds, private placements, limited partnerships, real estate, mortgages, private notes, and more. To find out what the IRS excludes from allowable IRA investments, you can refer to IRS Publication 590. Some common investments that are not allowed in your IRA are collectibles, life insurance, and most coins, with the exception of gold coins.

IRAs always require custodians. The government has appointed two classes of companies legally permitted to hold IRA assets and handle the accounting and reporting. The first class includes banks, trust companies, savings and loans, and credit unions. The second includes broker-dealers, mutual fund companies, and insurance companies. There are approximately twenty companies in the United States that can act as custodians for self-directed IRAs. Because these companies are not legally approved custodians, as defined by the IRS, they appoint a licensed institution to act as their "nominal" custodian.

To learn more about IRAs, you may wish to order IRS publication 590 or access it online at www.irs.gov/formpubs/index. Another site that offers guidance for IRA owners interested in investing in real estate is www.iraresource.com. To find official information about the codes that govern the establishment and use of IRAs, go to http://uscode.house.gov/usc.htm. To find custodians who can help you with setting up a self-directed IRA, here is a partial list of companies and their sites to investigate.

- American Church Trust Company (www.churchtrust.com)
- CNA Trust Corporation (www.cnatrust.com)
- First Trust Corporation (www.firsttrust.com)
- Lincoln Trust (www.lincolntrust.com)
- PENSCO Trust Company (www.pensco.com)
- Sterling Trust Company (www.sterling-trust.com)

The Tax-Free Education

If you have school-aged children or grandchildren, you may be interested in learning more about the education IRA. This account has no relationship to other IRAs; nor do contributions to an education IRA limit the amount that you can contribute to your other IRAs. The Taxpayer Relief Act of 1997 created this account, officially called the Coverdell Education Savings Account, to allow taxpayers to save tax-free dollars each year for a child's education. The assets in the account grow tax free and can be withdrawn for college costs tax free as well. You can open the account in your child's name but remain in control of the account.

Each year, you or anyone else can make contributions, which cannot total more than $2,000, until the child reaches 18 years of age. Similar to the Roth IRA, while your contributions are not deductible, withdrawals from the account are tax free, as long as the distributions are used for educational expenses and the beneficiary is under thirty years of age. If there is still money remaining after the beneficiary has finished college, you can roll the remaining monies into another education IRA for the benefit of another family member. Remember, anyone can contribute to the account – family members, friends, neighbors, and even the child himself.

Unlike other IRAs, contributions to an education IRA need not come from earned income. For example, daughters Kelly and Kelsey could each receive a $500 check from their uncle on their birthdays. Instead of spending the money at the mall, they could deposit the checks into their respective education IRAs. (Note: examples, while technically correct, may bear little resemblance to reality.)

Another beneficial wrinkle is that the IRS does not require you to use the money specifically for college expenses. As long as you use the money for qualifying educational expenses — whether you use it for elementary school, secondary school, or college — you can withdraw it tax free at any time. For example, assume that you start an education IRA for a toddler. You could later use the funds — which would have grown tax free — to fund an education at an expensive private school. No other type of account could offer you tax-free growth with that much flexibility.

Of course, there is nothing to say that you cannot have both an education IRA and a 529 Plan. A 529 plan is a state-operated investment plan that gives families a federal tax-free way to save money for college. Both education IRAs and 529 plans have their own advantages. The 529 plans allow for larger contributions (each state has its own plan and limitations). Moreover, the 529 plan does not place any restrictions on income, whereas to qualify for an education IRA, your adjusted gross income, assuming you are married, must be less than $220,000. Still, it is relatively easy to get around this restriction. Another family member, such as a grandparent, can set up the account, naming your child as the beneficiary.

So the 529 has its advantages, but the education IRA beats the 529 plan for a few reasons.

The education IRA is not restricted to college expenses only.
You can transfer the education IRA to another family member.

You have total control over the investments you make with an education IRA.

Let's examine the final advantage in more detail. In a 529 plan, the administrators of the plan control the investments. The money is all in stocks and bonds, with shifting asset allocation depending on the age of the child. For newborns, the allocation is typically 80 percent stocks and 20 percent bonds. At age ten, the mix may change to 40 percent stocks and 60 percent bonds. By the time a child has turned eighteen, the mix may be 10 percent stocks and 90 percent bonds.

Under such rigid formulations that completely ignore market cycles, there is no telling what the results will look like. What if you had started the plan in the year 2000? The plan would have invested 80 percent of your contributions in the market right at the peak. Years later, the value of your 529 plan would be less than your total dollars invested. At least with prepaid college plans — which I recommend if your state offers one — regardless of what the market does, you know that your child's college tuition will be paid.

What to Do Now

There is no way of knowing how high taxes will be in the future. While the trend has been toward lower federal income taxes, the actions of future administrations could reverse that trend. By the time you hope to reap the benefits of your investment planning, the tax code could be entirely revamped. It would seem reasonable, however, that the government will grandfather prior investments in tax-deferred and tax-free accounts. Therefore, you should act now to take advantage of these gifts. Here's what to do.

- Maximize your 401(k) contributions to reduce current income taxes and gain up to an immediate 35 percent return.
- If you only have a 401(k), open a Roth IRA and contribute what you can.
- If you have a traditional IRA, convert it to a Roth if you have the ability to pay the taxes due on the conversion and if your adjusted gross income is less than $100,000.
- If you would like to make real estate investments, look into setting up a self-directed IRA.
- Open an education IRA for your children or grandchildren.

Once you have set up accounts to protect as much future profits as possible, you can take the next step, which is to learn how to become an investor. To begin, you need a working knowledge of various investment vehicles and products. If your experience in markets is limited, you may find the amount of new information in the next chapter overwhelming. However, don't allow yourself to get bogged down. Skip ahead if you need to. You can always go back later and reread sections when you are ready to use those particular investment vehicles and products. Additionally, you may find it handy to take a few notes. Once you are ready, I invite you to report for duty at my Investor's Boot Camp.

5

How to Invest Like a Pro

I have enough money to last me the rest of my life, unless I buy something.[1]

~ Jackie Mason

It's easy to get caught up in the minutia of life and miss the big financial picture. That is why so many smart people never achieve financial independence. Here is the big picture: labor and capital make the world go around. Both produce a return. You can choose to contribute labor or contribute capital. The outcome is the same. On either investment, you receive a return that provides for your consumption needs. Therefore, why not choose to be a capitalist?

Chances are you have invested thousands of hours and years of your life learning how to become a laborer. Are you good at it? Congratulations! Now, let me ask you this: how much time have you devoted to learning how to be good capitalist? (For our purposes, I will use the term capitalist and investor interchangeably.) Regardless of your answer, my point is that you invested a lot of time learning to be a good laborer. Now you need to invest time learning to be a good capitalist (investor).

To profit from the coming inflation, you will need certain skills. In this chapter, you will learn how to use different kinds of investment vehicles and products. Some of the investment vehicles and products require a more in-depth knowledge of trading than I can give you in this chapter. If you are new to investing, don't worry. Many are easy to use and you will learn exactly what types of investments to make in later chapters. Here's exactly what you will learn in this chapter.

- Why mutual funds are for losers.
- How to make big money even in bear markets.
- How to inflation-proof your bond investments.
- How to invest in the stock market without risking any money.
- How to focus your investing with laserlike accuracy.
- How to leverage your stock positions without using margin.
- How to profit from the dollar's inevitable decline.
- How to maximize your profits from rising prices in energy, metals, and food.

Why Mutual Funds Are for Losers

Ninety-five million Americans own mutual funds. Are you one of them? If so, your mutual fund is either open-ended or closed. When you invest money in an open-ended fund, the fund issues shares to you and then uses your money to buy more stocks; when you liquidate a position, they do the opposite: redeem the shares, sell the stock, and send back your money. Each day, the fund determines the value of its holdings and calculates a net asset value (NAV) for the fund, which is then divided by the number of outstanding shares to determine the NAV per share. Much like the price of a stock, the NAV is the price at which you buy or sell.

In contrast, with a closed-end fund, the number of shares remains fixed. You cannot buy shares from the fund as you can with an open-ended fund. Instead, you must buy the shares from someone else who owns them, just as you would a stock. While companies first issue shares through an initial public offering, further buying and selling of shares takes place on exchanges. The share price is not necessarily the same as the fund's NAV. Because supply and demand determines the price, the share price may be higher or lower than the NAV. When it is lower, the fund trades at a discount to its NAV; when the share price is higher, it trades at a premium.

The first mutual funds introduced to the public were load funds. These funds charged whopping, front-end sales commissions, known as loads — usually about 8.5 percent of the money you invested. It would normally take a year or more before you could expect to regain your initial investment. Later, the industry introduced no-load funds, which you could buy without paying a sales fee. After a few years, it was clear that no-load funds performed just as well, if not better, than most load funds. However, for many years, commissions on the sale of load funds had been the bread-and-butter for stockbrokers, insurance salesmen, and financial planners.

While mutual funds have many advantages over individual stocks, as you learned earlier, mutual funds generally underperform the major stock averages. Fund managers are not dumb, but they simply cannot match the performance of indexes that do not have to pay salaries, overhead, commissions, and bid-ask spreads. Therefore, if I could buy all the stocks in the S&P 500 and you bought a mutual fund, there is a 90 percent chance that I would achieve a superior performance. Is it possible to buy all the stocks in a stock market index? Yes, you can buy all the stocks represented by popular stock market indexes by buying an index fund.

A Better Way to Invest in the Stock Market

Vanguard launched the first index fund in 1976. Called the Vanguard 500 Index Fund, it tracks the S&P 500. Today, there are numerous index funds offered by many different companies. A major advantage of index funds is that, because stock selections simply attempt to duplicate the composition of the index, no costly stock research is required. Because an index such as the S&P 500 is capitalization weighted, the fund must put more money into the stocks that have larger capitalizations and less money into the stocks with smaller capitalizations. Other than that, the funds are unmanaged.

When Vanguard first launched its index fund, it was ridiculed. However, nearly half of the mutual funds in existence at that time no longer exist today. Meanwhile, the Vanguard 500 Index Fund has become the largest fund in the world with $120 billion under management. In 1992, Vanguard introduced the Vanguard Total Stock Market Index Fund, designed to track the broader Wilshire 5000.

In conclusion, professional money managers do better than non-professionals, but even professional money managers underperform stock market indexes. Therefore, if you must invest in the stock market, the best way to do it is to put your money in one of Vanguard's index funds. Statistics indicate that you will do better than most bank trust departments, professional mutual fund managers, and individual investors. Moreover, your stock market investing will require very little time and effort.

Given my bearish orientation toward the stock market, you may wonder why I have taken the time to discuss index funds. Here's why. First, I have no idea when you will be reading this book. I received a call yesterday from a woman who had just finished reading Timing the Market, a book I had written over twenty years ago. The second reason is that, to appreciate fully the investment products that follow, you need to understand index funds. Finally, many of you will remain bullish and want to keep some funds in the market. If you do, index funds are your best buy.

How to Make Money in Bear Markets

In the past, if you thought that the stock market was headed for a rough patch, you would switch your money out of mutual funds and into a money market fund. After you sat out the bear market safely in T-bills, you would switch back into your mutual funds after the next bull market got underway. Wouldn't it be great if, instead of waiting on the sidelines, you could actually make money during the bear market? Well, thanks to the people at Rydex and Profunds, you can.

Each of these companies offers funds that make money when the stock market goes down. They are called — not unexpectedly — bear market funds. We will begin with Rydex. You can invest in one of the Rydex funds through your discount broker for as little as $2,500 ($2,000 if the account is an IRA). If you expect the price of the S&P 500 to

Table 5.1 Rydex Bear Funds

Ursa Fund	RYURX	Inverse of S&P 500
Tempest Fund	RYTPX	Twice the inverse of S&P 500
Arktos Fund	RYAIX	Inverse of NASDAQ 100
Venture Fund	RYVNX	Twice the inverse of NASDAQ 100

Table 5.2 Profunds Bear Funds

Bear Fund	BRPIX	Inverse of S&P 500
Ultra Bear Fund	URPIX	Twice the inverse of S&P 500
Short OTC Fund	SOPIX	Inverse of NASDAQ 100
Ultra Short	USPIX	Twice the inverse of NASDAQ 100
Ultra Short Dow 30 Fund	UWPIX	Twice the inverse of the DOW

decline, buy their Ursa fund (RYURX), which is the inverse of the S&P 500. If you are extremely bearish and confident of your analysis, buy the Tempest fund (RYTPX), which is leveraged to produce a return twice the inverse of the S&P 500 index. If you are more bearish on the tech sector, buy the Arktos fund (RYAIX), which is the inverse of the NASDAQ 100. To leverage that bet, buy the Venture Fund (RYVNX), which is two times the inverse of the NASDAQ 100.

The second fund family for you to investigate is the Profunds family, which also offers a large selection of bear funds. To short the S&P 500, buy the Bear fund (BRPIX). To leverage your bet, buy the Ultra Bear (URPIX), which is twice the inverse of the S&P 500. To short the NASDAQ, buy the Short OTC fund (SOPIX). To leverage that bet, buy the Ultra Short (SOPIX). Profunds also offers a way to short the Dow. Buy the Ultra Short Dow 30 Fund (UWPIX), which is twice the inverse of the Dow.

A third way to short the S&P 500 is to short the SPDR (pronounced spider; symbol SPY), which is an exchange-traded fund (ETF) that mimics the S&P 500. You will learn a lot more about ETFs shortly. For the time being, just know that shorting the SPDRs is another option that will allow you to get short quickly because no uptick is required to sell. Unlike Rydex and Profunds products, which you "buy," you cannot use

Table 5.3 Rydex and Profunds Bear Bond Funds

Juno Fund	RYJUX	Inverse of 30-year bond
Rising Rates Fund	RRPIX	125% of inverse of 30-year bond

the SPDR to short the market if you are trading in your IRA because you are not allowed to sell short. Again, that highlights the beauty of Rydex and Profunds products. How else can you use your IRA to bet against the market?

If you believe that inflation will be higher in the future, you must also believe that interest rates on long-term bonds will be higher as well. If investors anticipate future inflation, they will demand a higher return to compensate for their diminished purchasing power when they redeem their bonds. There is no other way it can be. Inflation equals higher long-term interest rates; higher long-term interest rates equal lower bond prices.

Once again, the people at Rydex and Profunds have come to our rescue. At Rydex, you can buy the Juno fund (RYJUX), which acts as a proxy for shorting the thirty-year bond. At Profunds, you can buy the Rising Rates fund (RRPIX). Learn more about Rydex at www.rydex-funds.com and Profunds at www.profunds.com.

How to Inflation-Proof Your Bond Investments

What if you owned a bond that went up in value as inflation increased? Well, you can by purchasing Treasury Inflation Protection Securities (TIPS). Just like other government bonds, you can buy and sell TIPS on the open market. The difference between TIPS and regular government bonds is that these instruments were designed to protect your returns from being eroded by inflation. For example, if inflation (measured by the CPI) rose 3 percent next year, the face value of the bond would also rise 3 percent.

Follow this example. You buy a $10,000 TIPS with a coupon rate of 5 percent. If that were a regular bond, it would pay you $250 in interest every six months. With a TIPS, if inflation were 3 percent, the face value of your bond would rise to $10,300. Since the coupon remains fixed at 5 percent, you would receive \$515 in interest that year, paid in two semi-annual payments of \$257.50 each. More importantly, the face value of your bond would have increased by \$300.

Before getting too excited, remember that when the government gives you something with one hand, it often takes it away with the other. Such is the case here. The IRS ruled that you not only have to pay taxes on the interest you receive but also on the inflation adjustment to your principle. In our example, you would pay income tax on \$815.

If you are worried about deflation, however, you should not buy TIPS. In that case, the face value would adjust downwards by the amount of the deflation. Happily, once the TIPS reaches maturity, the government will pay the face value even if it has been downwardly adjusted due to deflation.

Another advantage of TIPS is that, should interest rates rise as would likely occur in an inflationary environment, the value will not fall as much as other bonds. On the other hand, because of that, TIPS pay less interest than ten-year Treasuries. Recently, while ten-year Treasuries yielded 4 percent, TIPS yielded only $3\frac{1}{2}$ percent. With this differential, a simple calculation shows you that if inflation averaged more than 1 percent per year over the next ten years, the TIPS would be the superior investment. Here's a tip: an easy way to buy TIPS is to invest in the Vanguard Inflation-protected Securities Fund (VIPX), which is a mutual fund that invests in TIPS.

How to Invest in the Stock Market without Risk

What if you could invest in the stock market without risking any money? If that sounds impossible, I can guarantee that it is not. An investment vehicle exists that allows you to get every dollar you invested back if the stock market goes down, but make as much as you would have otherwise made if the stock market goes up. The instruments, offered through Merrill Lynch, are called MITTS, which stands for Market Index Target-Term Securities. You can buy MITTS that allow you to invest in many of the major stock market indexes.

Assume that you wish to invest \$10,000 in the stock market because you are bullish over the near term. You could buy a MITTS that replicates the S&P 500 with an expiration date two years in the future. To ensure that your money is protected even if the market is much lower in two years, the brokerage firm would use a portion of your $10,000 to buy $10,000 of zero coupon bonds that would mature at the same date as your MITTS. Because these bonds are sold at a discount (like a CD), the brokerage firm has money left over. With that money, it buys call options on the S&P 500 Index. You can choose the expiration date of your MITTS and even trade in and out of them like stocks.

As long as you do not pay more than par (the original price of the MITTS), you cannot lose any money. Moreover, you can make just as much as if you had put your money in an S&P 500 Index fund. Of course, it goes without saying that, if the market goes down, you will only get back the money that you paid. You will have given up opportunity costs and lost some purchasing power during that period. However, that is a small price to pay to protect your investment completely.

How to Focus Your Investing with Laserlike Accuracy

Earlier in this chapter, you learned both about closed-end funds and about index funds. An ETF is a closed-end fund that operates like an index fund, but with even lower expenses. ETFs offer far more flexibility than mutual funds. They allow you to focus on specific sectors and industries to take advantage of market movements caused by the coming inflation. Here are their key advantages over mutual funds.

- You can trade ETFs at any time of the day, just like stocks; you can only purchase mutual funds at the close.
- ETF annual fees are lower, averaging as low as .09 percent of assets compared to 1.4 percent with mutual funds.
- You can buy ETFs on margin; you cannot margin mutual fund purchases.
- Many ETFs have options, which allow you to hedge positions or speculate with less money; mutual funds do not have options.

We can learn a bit more about ETFs by simply understanding what ETF stands for.

- "E" stands for exchange. That means that ETFs are listed like any other stock with a symbol and bid and ask price.
- "T" stands for traded. ETFs are repriced every fifteen seconds and you can trade them all day long, just likes stocks.
- "F" stands for fund. An ETF is like a fund in that it is composed of a basket of stocks. The basket may simulate an index such as the S&P 500 Index, the NASDAQ, or the Dow Jones Industrial Average. Additionally, ETFs exist for virtually every sector of the market. You can even trade ETFs that represent the stocks of different countries.

There are three popular families of ETFs: Holders (Merrill Lynch), iShares (Barclays), and SPDRs (Standard and Poors). Together, these companies offer ETFs that mimic fifty-one different industry sectors as well as eight others that mimic broad market indexes. By the time you read this book, you can expect to find even more ETFs because more are being created all the time.

Investors often spend too much time trying to pick stocks and too little time deciding what sectors, countries, and types of stocks to buy. Why bother when 95 percent of performance can be attributed to asset allocation? When you attempt to stock pick, you are competing with thousands of analysts who are doing the same. There is little public information that could give you a unique advantage. Not only is asset allocation easier than stock picking, its rewards are greater as well.

The following table lists eight of the major index ETFs, all of which emulate a particular market index.

Sector ETFs let you slice and dice the market so that you can focus your investing with laserlike accuracy. There are more than fifty different sector ETFs and more are being added all the time. Regardless of what the overall market is doing, some sectors will be going up in price and others will be going down. Here are some of the basic sectors and ETFs that mimic their price movements.

Many ETFs exist that allow you to drill down further and focus your investing to an even greater degree. For example, you could buy all the

Table 5.4 Major Index ETFs

SPY	S&P 500 SPDR	Tracks the S&P 500 Index
QQQQ	NASDAQ 100 Tracking Stock	Tracks 100 largest NASDAQ stocks
DIA	Diamonds	Tracks the Dow Jones Industrial Average
MDY	S&P MidCap 400 SPDRs	Tracks the S&P MidCap 400 Index
IWM	iShares Russell 2000	Tracks the Russell 2000 Index, a popular benchmark for mid-cap and small-cap companies
EFA	iShares MSCI EAFE	Tracks the index of the same name, which represents the top non-U.S. large capitalization companies
VTI	Total Stock Market Vipers	Tracks the Wilshire 5000 broad market index, a good proxy for the U.S. economy
IJR	iShares SmallCap 600	Tracks the performance of 600 small capitalization companies in the U.S

Chinese companies that are listed on the New York Stock Exchange by purchasing shares in the PowerShares Golden Dragon Halter USX Portfolio (PGJ). Possibly more relevant to those of us who expect future inflation is the streetTracks Gold Trust (GLD). For the first time ever, the public can now own shares backed by physical gold. Before this ETF, to own gold you would need to either buy physical bullion (inconvenient) or buy shares in a gold mining stock (not an exact proxy).

International ETFs consist of groups of companies in countries outside the United States. For example, instead of buying just U.S. healthcare companies, you could buy a global Healthcare ETF. The same can be said of energy, financials, telecommunications, and technology. You can also invest in entire regions such as Asia, Europe, the Pacific Rim, Latin America, and in emerging markets. Country funds, known as WEBS, let you invest in individual countries – twenty-two at last count.

ETFs allow you to place bets both on interest rates and on real estate. If you believe that interest rates on long-term bonds will move higher, you could profit by selling short the iShares Lehman 20+ Year Treasury Bond Fund (TLT). You can also play the real estate market, either up or

Table 5.5 Major Sectors and Corresponding ETFs

Basic Materials	XLB	SPDR
Consumer Cyclicals	XLY	SPDR
Consumer Non-Cyclicals	XLP	SPDR
Energy	XLE	SPDR
Financial	XLF	SPDR
Healthcare	IYH	iShares
Industrial	XLI	SPDR
Real Estate	IYR	iShares
Technology	XLK	SPDR
Telecommunications	IYZ	iShares

down, by buying or shorting an REIT ETF. The iShares DJ U.S. Real Estate ETF (IYR) is a good way to do that.

How to Leverage Your Stock Positions without Using Margin

LEAPS is the common acronym for long-term equity anticipation securities. In reality, they are simply stock options that have a longer expiration, and that is their big advantage over regular stock options. Options offer a way to control a specific number of shares of stock with a limited amount of money. With options, you risk only the money that you pay for the option.

LEAPS expirations can go out as much as one, two, or three years rather than just nine months. Because LEAPS become available for trading in July, the longest you can actually hold LEAPS is two and one-half years. As they come closer to expiration (about six months out), LEAPS are no longer LEAPS. Their symbols change and they become regular options.

LEAPS offer many advantages. One of them is that you can leverage your stock position without borrowing on margin. You will never receive a margin call and you can never lose more than the cost of the LEAP. Typically, you can buy the LEAP for less than half the price of the stock, which leaves you more capital for trading.

LEAPS are a product that you can invest in, as opposed to options, which are short-term in nature and require a trading mentality. However, in order to buy LEAPS, you should be familiar with the mechanics of option trading. Before attempting to use options and LEAPS in your own trading, take the time to educate yourself more thoroughly on the subject. A good place to start is the Chicago Board of Options site (www.cboe.com), which offers a great deal of free information for the beginner.

LEAPS have three primary advantages.

1. You may qualify for long-term capital gains.
2. You can leverage your stock positions without using margin.
3. Time premium decay is minimal compared to options.

How to Maximize Your Profit from
Rising Prices of Energy, Natural Resources, and Food

I know that you have heard of the futures markets and commodities, but for most people, it gets a little blurry after that. I spent almost two decades intimately involved in the commodity markets — as a private trader, money manager, system developer, and educator. I wrote three books and numerous articles on trading. I began trading commodities in the late 1970s, when I learned that, instead of buying physical gold as I had planned, I could buy gold futures contracts. With the leverage available in the commodity markets, I could control about twenty times as much gold as I could have otherwise afforded.

I took the plunge and the rest, as they say, is history. I made so much money my first week in the markets that I jettisoned a career as a systems analyst, for which I had spent the last six years of my life preparing. I did not regret it for one moment. Although I experienced many ups and downs along the way, I cannot think of a more exciting way to make a living than by trading (okay, maybe being a rock star).

I will not bore you with personal history. Instead, I will give you a brief overview of commodity trading so that you will have enough information to pursue the subject in more detail if you have an interest. First, let me clarify a minor point of terminology that often confuses people. Commodities refer to physical markets like gold, silver, copper, crude oil, soybeans, wheat, lumber, coffee, sugar, and so forth. Futures refer to financial markets, like T-bonds, the Eurodollar, and the S&P 500 Index. While not technically correct, traders tend to use both terms interchangeably and I use them interchangeably as well.

When I began trading commodities, the stock market was in a bear market that had been going on since I was in Little League. There was not a lot of public interest in the stock market. Because of the inflation in the 1970s, however, almost all commodities were enjoying major bull markets. Those investors who were adventurous enough to try something new made a lot of money. When the bull market in stocks got under way in the 1980s and inflation began retreating, the backs of the commodity bull markets were broken and interest in commodities waned. The industry remained vibrant during the bull market in stocks only because the exchanges introduced new products — currency futures, interest rate futures, and stock index futures. Traders who knew how to trade commodities could make a lot of money in these new markets because they could apply leverage to big trends in stock, bond, and currency markets.

Commodity markets were created back in the 1800s so that commercial interests (farmers, for example) could hedge their crops. Instead of waiting until their crops were harvested to get paid, they could sell part of their crops (to be delivered in the future) at today's price. If the price were lower in the future, they would have already locked in part of the sale of their crop at a higher price; if prices were higher, they might have wished that they had waited. Most business that use commodity markets — such as farmers, oil companies, and mining companies — run more smoothly if they hedge future production throughout the course of the year rather than take a chance that prices could be lower at the time they are ready to bring their goods to market.

Just as the big money in stocks is made in bull markets, the same can be said of commodity markets. In addition, commodity markets tend to exhibit an inverse price relationship to stocks. When stocks are in a bull market, commodity markets are lethargic; when stocks are in a bear market, many commodity markets are roaring. It does not take a genius to understand why. Inflation calls the tune. When inflation is high, so are interest rates. Investors flee stocks for the safer and more attractive yields of bonds. Additionally, commodities benefit as investors race to buy physical goods that they know will cost more in the future.

The global demand for commodities is beginning to outstrip supply. Relative to FOREX and the stock and bond markets, commodity markets are rather small by comparison. If investors find that their stocks and bonds are not producing the kinds of returns that they expected and they discover commodities as they did in the 1970s, there is a strong likelihood that we will see mega trends develop that dwarf even what we witnessed in the 1970s. In other words, smart traders will make fortunes in commodities in the years ahead just as they did in the 1970s.

The supply of commodities has not kept pace with the tremendous growth of wealth (fiat money). Additionally, if institutional money managers divert even a tiny fraction of their investment portfolios to commodities, the effect on the markets would be startling. Moreover, as you will see in the next chapter, China is buying physical resource companies as fast as they can. They are trying to control many commodities at the source, knowing that their demand will increase as their multidecade industrialization process continues.

While I believe that commodities will offer tremendous rewards for investors and traders in the coming decade, a stern caveat is in order. In one of my previous books, I said that trading commodities was like driving a fast car on an oily road. My opinion has not changed. During my nearly two decades in the business, it was discouraging to see how many people lose money.

Commodity markets are difficult to trade for a host of reasons. Leverage, of course, is one factor. Underfunded accounts is another. Beginning traders believe that, by starting with a small amount, they are reducing risk. In fact, just the opposite is true. A small account forces a trader out of trades due to margin calls and reduces his staying power. Overtrading is also a major problem. Unless your brokerage firm offers rock bottom commissions, frequent trading amounts to giving most of your money to the brokerage firm.

In order to make money by trading commodities, you must employ a trading system so that you can eliminate emotion-based trading. All professional traders employ trading systems. For the most part, the systems are computerized and the manager's function is simply to follow the system. I was a systems analyst prior to entering financial markets, and system design was my forte. It took me ten years to design my system (PPS), but the results were worth the effort.

Convinced that small traders needed to employ systems to win in the commodity markets, I spent years teaching seminars, writing articles, and even books in an attempt to educate the trading public. Unfortunately, I found that it took most traders at least three years before they came to the realization that to be successful they would need to follow a trading system. By then, probably only one out of a hundred beginning traders was still in the markets.

If you do decide to trade commodities, I humbly recommend my book, *Curtis Arnold's PPS Trading System*. Most of what I learned during fifteen years of full-time study made it into the book. Additionally, I would advise that you seek out and read as much as you can about the psychology of trading. Finally — and this applies to trading in all markets — money management is the most crucial aspect of successful trading.

Good money management means never allowing a trade to turn into a large loss. You may get away with it once or even twice, but eventually that type of trading behavior will be your Achilles' heel. Successful traders are ruthless about cutting losses quickly. I once took seventeen losses in a row. I was able to do that because I cut losses very quickly and never let a loss get out of control. Furthermore, I had complete faith in my system because I had tested it over thousands of trials. Given that its win/loss ratio was about 1:3, I knew that after a thousand trials (like rolls of the dice), a run of seventeen losses was to be expected. The system recovered nicely, and because average wins averaged seven times the dollar amount of average losses, the system went on to make a great deal of money.

Not only was it difficult to convince beginning traders that they needed to employ a system, it was even more difficult to get them to follow a system once they had one. It is not that these people were morons. Following a system, even a great system, is extremely difficult. All systems go through drawdowns (losing periods when your account decreases in value). When that occurs, it is human nature to want to try something different. You might conclude that successful commodity trading is extremely difficult. You would be right. However, smart traders will make fortunes in commodities during the next decade. If commodity trading is not your cup of tea, however, fear not. In the next chapter, you will learn other ways to make money from big commodity moves.

My Thoughts on Leverage

While I do not borrow money to buy consumer items, I have no problem borrowing money to make more money — that is, for investing. Without the ability to borrow money, I could not have bought my first house, made real estate investments, or invested in commodities. Leverage, used wisely, is a good thing, and can mean the difference between mediocrity and great success.

The more you can borrow, the more you can make on your investments. When you buy real estate, banks will loan 80 to 100 percent of the purchase price. Leverage is what makes real estate such a good investment. For example, assume that you buy a house for $250,000 with a down payment of $25,000. The house goes up in value 10 percent. Because of the leverage, the return on your investment was 100 percent. In the stock market, you could buy $250,000 of eBay stock using 50 percent margin. If the stock's price goes up 10 percent, you make a return of 20 percent. The difference between the two gains is phenomenal. All things being equal, you would make five times as much money with the real estate investment because of the difference in leverage.

To continue with the analogy, assume that you go into the futures market and buy $250,000 of gold. Because the margin requirement is only 4 percent, you only need to invest $10,000. If the price of gold goes up 10 percent, your return on investment is 250 percent. What if you buy $250,000 of Swiss francs in the FOREX market? The margin in the FOREX

Table 5.6 Comparison of Leverage among Various Assets

Type of Asset	Cost of Asset	Money Needed to Control Asset	Hypothetical Appreciation	Return on Investment
Stocks	$250,000	$250,000	10%	10%
Stocks margined	$250,000	$125,000	10%	20%
Real estate	$250,000	$25,000	10%	100%
Futures	$250,000	$10,000	10%	250%
FOREX	$250,000	$2500	10%	1000%

is 1 percent, so you only need to invest $2500. If the Swiss franc goes up in value by 10 percent against the U.S. dollar, your return on investment is 1000 percent.

In summary, all markets move both up and down; they have trends because of supply and demand pressures, often resulting from geopolitical events and geopolitical trends. Sometimes, the events happen unexpectedly and the markets react chaotically. More often, however, it is possible to spot these geopolitical trends as they develop and predict the outcome on markets.

Therefore, if we can identify the trends that are occurring and make educated guesses as to what effects those trends will have on markets — that is, prices of things — we can position ourselves to make a lot of money. There are many kinds of markets, however, and each has its vagaries, rules, and most importantly, leverage available. By knowing where we can get the most leverage, we do not have to be rich to play; we can place our bets using other peoples' money (OPM). In our example, we examined four investments: one in stocks, one in real estate, one in futures, and one in the FOREX. Each investment increased in value by 10 percent. Our returns were 20 percent in stocks, 100 percent in real estate, 250 percent in futures, and 1000 percent in the FOREX. You can see that which casino you play in is very important.

To be fair, however, I should point out that leverage can work against you, multiplying your losses to the same degree as your potential profits. When you take on a position that is highly leveraged, you can be right in the long run but forced to liquidate your position if the market goes against you in the short run. Determining how much to leverage is tricky even for professionals and in the end becomes a personal choice. However, the following rules will help to keep you out of trouble regardless of how much leverage you decide to employ.

The Four Tenets of Successful Trading

Regardless of what markets you decide to trade, you will enjoy greater success as a trader or investor if you learn to follow a few simple rules. This is how I trade and how most great traders have made their fortunes. Here are the rules.

1. Trade with the trend.
2. Cut losses short.
3. Let profits run.
4. Use good money management.

The first rule is a very important one. The old trading adage "Don't fight the tape" conveys the same advice. You can determine the trend in any number of ways. The easiest way is to take a chart of whatever you want to buy, hold it up to your five-year-old and ask, "Is this going up or down?" You do not need to overanalyze.

The second rule, "Cut losses short," simply means that you should not allow yourself to get into a situation where you will have to take a big loss. Again, it's not rocket science; if you're losing money, get out of the position.

The third rule, "Let profits run," means that you should not be too quick to take profits. Generally, trends last longer than you expect. The "trend is your friend" so give it the benefit of the doubt.

The fourth rule, "Use good money management," means that you should not go overboard on any one position. Divide your money up into portions and only risk a predetermined amount on each trade.

Play it Again, Sam

For those of you who have not traded financial markets before, this chapter may have been challenging. Therefore, before going any further, a summary might be in order.

- We all begin as laborers. However, laborers are expendable regardless of rank. You can choose to become a capitalist and let your money work for you by learning to be a successful investor.
- Most people invest by way of mutual funds. However, mutual funds underperform the market. Index funds are a better choice for funds earmarked for the market.
- Bear market funds can make you money even when the stock market is going down and interest rates are rising.
- ETFs give you the ability to focus on individual sectors and market industries, as well as regions and countries.
- LEAPS give you a way to leverage your bets in many popular stocks without experiencing the rapid time premium decay that you would with traditional options.
- FOREX trading offers you extreme leverage on foreign currencies.
- Futures markets offer you extreme leverage on commodities and other financial instruments.

Congratulations! Now that you have learned *how* to invest, you are ready to learn *what* to buy. In the next chapter, you are going to see why, in order to profit from the coming inflation, you need to invest in commodities – especially oil. I see a worried look on your face. Relax; let me assure you that I am not sending you off to the trading pits in Chicago or New York. There are easier and safer ways to profit from the commodity bull. I have five action plans all laid out for you. Now turn the page to learn how to ride that commodity bull without getting gored.

OIL

6

How to Profit from Rising Commodity Prices

Commodities tend to zig when the equity markets zag."[1]

~ Jim Rogers

I consider myself fortunate to have written a book about the stock and commodity markets early in my trading career. One of the less appreciated benefits of writing a book is the vast knowledge you acquire by doing the research. This knowledge laid the foundation for my trading success. If I were to advise a young investor today, I would counsel him to read as many books as possible about the great traders of the twentieth century who dedicated their lives to understanding markets.

One thing he would find is that these traders had a profound knowledge of commodities as well as stocks and plied both trades with equal alacrity. They learned that if one were to make trading and investing a lifelong affair, he would encounter many bull and bear markets, panics, and crashes. Only through a thorough study of market history can the investor hope to appreciate that such is the nature of markets, and then prepare to invest accordingly. Furthermore, because the average investor fails to understand market cycles, he often zigs just when he should zag.

The Commodity Cycle

Both stock and commodity markets exhibit a very powerful cycle lasting approximately seventeen to eighteen years. For purists, the stock market cycle is slightly over eighteen years, while the commodity cycle is closer to seventeen years. However, for practical purposes, understanding that the cycles are approximately the same length will suffice. More important is the fact that these cycles are negatively correlated – that is, when stocks are in bull markets, commodities are in bear markets, and vice versa.

For example, if we were to examine the twentieth century, we would find that commodities exhibited a bull market from 1906 to 1923, while stocks languished. Subsequently, the stock market exploded and commodities entered a bear market. The next major bull market in commodities began in 1933 and lasted until 1953. Subsequently, low commodity prices and benign inflation rates in the 1950s fostered the stock market bull during the 1950s and into the 1960s.

The next major commodity bull market began in 1968 and lasted until 1982, a period during which the stock market remained locked in a trading range. You may remember that 1982 marked the start of the great bull market in stocks, which lasted eighteen years, during which time commodities fell out of favor. The new commodity bull market began in 1999. If history is a guide, we might expect this new bull market to last until approximately 2016, with its greatest gains occurring in the last part of the market cycle.

Successful investors always begin by attempting to determine the phase of the current market cycle. In commodities, the task is a little more difficult. All commodities, given their diversity, have their own individual cycles. For example, the fundamentals that govern copper production have little in common with the fundamentals governing the

Table 6.1 20th Century Commodity Bull Markets

1906 – 1923	17 years
1933 – 1953	20 years
1968 – 1982	14 years
1999 – (2016)	(17 years)

soybean crop. Commodity sectors such as metals, energy, and grains exhibit their own cycles. Moreover, the prices of individual commodities within the sectors march to their own drummers.

Given the diversity among commodity markets, you may wonder how the dominant seventeen-year commodity cycle can influence all of the disparate commodities. I would ask you to remember that the world's commodities are the basic inputs to production. When the costs of these inputs are low, the profits of commodity producers suffer. Their industries do not attract capital and they are not anxious to expand production. At the same time, manufacturers' costs are down, making them more profitable. Where would you rather invest? You would rather invest in the manufacturers, of course. Thus, the manufacturers' stock prices rise and the stock market does well.

In the next phase of the cycle, manufacturers expand production and require more raw input (commodities). Demand begins to overwhelm supply so the prices of commodities are bid up. The rising costs of commodities result in two simultaneous effects. First, the manufacturers' profit margins shrink and capital stops flowing into their stocks. Second, because the commodity producers cannot keep up with demand, they increase production, which might take the form of buying more farmland for crops, investing in new mines for metals, or investing in new drilling rigs for oil exploration. Of course, it takes years for the commodity industry to ramp up capacity enough to meet the increased demand. All the while, commodity prices trend higher because the supply/demand equation is out of balance.

Eventually, however, the new capital flowing to the commodity producers results in enough production to meet the increased demand. How-

Table 6.2 Phases of the Commodity Cycle

Phase 1	Commodity prices are low; stock prices are high because the costs of inputs are low. Result: Manufacturers expand and demand more raw materials.
Phase 2	The demand for raw materials pushes commodity prices higher. Result: High commodity prices generate profits for commodity producers and they expand production. Meanwhile, high raw material prices squeeze profits of manufacturers, and their stock prices decline.
Phase 3	Commodity prices fall because increased production has caused an oversupply and manufacturers, who are no longer expanding, require less raw materials. (Return to Phase 1)

ever, markets rarely exhibit the precise efficiency that would allow supplies to meet demand exactly. More often, commodity producers will go overboard and produce too much. In the years that it took commodity producers to gear up, demand most likely fell due to higher prices and the public seeking substitution.

Substitution means that there is a limit to how much one will pay for something. If the price is too high, you will spend your money on something else. For example, you might pay $1 for a candy bar, but not $10; you might pay $15 for a steak, but not $150; you might pay $5,000 for a diamond engagement ring, but not $50,000. Therefore, just as commodity producers are spending millions gearing up to meet today's demand, future demand could be much lower.

As prices eventually plummet due to decreased demand and increased supply, commodity producers suffer while manufacturers now have the opportunity to increase their profit margins. Therefore, these powerful dominant cycles alternate, first favoring stocks (manufacturers) and then favoring commodities (producers of the inputs to manufacturing).

We are now in the early stages of major bull markets in commodities, based on the proven supply/demand cycles shown to exist for over one hundred years. Commodity prices are rising and inflationary pressures will mount. I spotted the first article attesting to that in the *Star Telegram* on January 8, 2005. It was entitled "Consumers feeling pinch of inflation."

After a decade of relatively tame prices, consumers are starting to feel the 'ouch' of inflation as the cost of everything from coffee, candy and home appliances is marching higher. It's not a sharp pain yet, and some call it hardly noticeable. But with some companies such as Procter & Gamble Co., Hershey Foods Corp. and Whirlpool Corp. passing along the higher prices they pay for raw materials to their customers, it's beginning to get attention from people who shop in grocery, appliance and department stores . . . the supply chain, which seems to have absorbed most of the higher costs, may be starting to pass those costs on. Analysts say a slowly improving economy is giving producers more confidence to raise prices, especially as excess inventories dwindle and commodities, from green coffee to oil, stay at elevated prices."[2]

It seems that there is a time for every season, and that we have now entered the season for commodities. I hope that you will have read this book early enough to prosper from this cycle. Remember, however, that the majority of the gains from the 18-year stock market cycle came in the last three years of the cycle. Prices in market cycles tend to start slowly and pick up steam along the way, finally ending in a stampede that brings prices to unsustainable levels.

You can be certain that there will be plenty of opportunities to get aboard this bull market because there will be major setbacks in prices throughout the course of the cycle. During the last commodity boom, which lasted from 1968 to 1982, prices moved up for a few years and then lost over half their value. They recovered some, move sideways for about five years, and finally spiked over 100 percent near the end of the cycle.

I do not anticipate an easy ride during this commodity bull market either. While we know that worldwide supply/demand factors look favorable for commodities for some time, the first initial setback could be caused by China. As you know, China's recent growth rate is unsustainable. Economies grow in fits and starts and China's economy is no different. As this book is being written, China is attempting to slow its growth to prevent inflation. A more moderate growth rate will benefit not only China, but also the rest of the world, which has become dependent on China's demand for its products.

Some economists worry that China could experience a hard landing — meaning that the slowdown would be more pronounced than planned. If that happens, China's demand for commodities will contract sharply and we could see sharp price setbacks in many commodity markets. If that were to occur, it would offer an excellent buying opportunity. China will quickly recover and its demand for commodities will continue to increase.

The China Factor

During the last commodity bull market in the 1970s, China was not a significant factor. The sleeping giant's economy was not growing rapidly, as it is today. Additionally, their economy was more or less self-contained. Now, they are active bidders on the world's markets for all significant commodities — oil, metals, and foodstuffs. China consumes more copper and steel than any other country in the world and is second in oil consumption. Therefore, expect China's insatiable appetite for commodities and all raw materials to fuel the current commodity boom.

With 1.3 billion people (more than four times the population of the United States) and its economy growing at a pace of 8 to 10 percent per year, China has been called the world's mouth. That was not always the case. China is relatively rich in natural resources and until recently was a major exporter of commodities. Now, however, their enormous population, which grows more prosperous each day, and their burgeoning economy requires more commodities and natural resources than China has. Their growth in infrastructure, factories, housing, and automobiles is draining the world's supply of metals and minerals. Meanwhile, as the population's income rises, individuals eat more meat, and chicken and cattle require more corn feed. The Chinese are also eating more candy, prompting an increase of sugar imports. While the growth in China is the primary factor driving commodity and natural resource consumption, growth throughout Asia adds even more demand.

The Mother of All Commodities

Because oil is the world's largest commodity, we will begin to look for ways to profit from the great commodity boom by first examining opportunities from the secular trend of higher energy prices. As you will see, unlike many of the other commodity markets, investing in oil is extremely easy. Let's first briefly review the fundamentals.

To begin, we know that demand for oil is outstripping supplies. As China demands more oil because of industrialization as well as more cars, trucks, and airplanes, the price of oil can only go higher. However, in addition to positive supply/demand fundamentals, oil is a political commodity and OPEC can easily disrupt its supply at any time. Finally, more so than any other commodity, the price of oil is vulnerable to terrorism and world conflicts.

Regardless of all the positives on the side of higher energy prices, it is important to remember that no market is a one-way street. The price of oil is cyclical, with bull markets averaging about three years. Additionally, because of rising prices, oil companies are frantically searching for oil. New discoveries and new technologies could cause setbacks for oil prices along the way. Finally, a worldwide recession could potentially stall the rise in energy consumption. It is important to recognize setbacks as temporary, and to view price declines as opportunities to invest.

The most direct and most leveraged way to take advantage of higher energy prices is to buy crude oil, heating oil, and natural gas futures. However, due to the great risk, unless you are an experienced commodity trader, you may wish to consider other approaches. A safer approach would be to invest in shares of companies that profit from higher oil prices. Those would include major oil companies, oil service companies, and exploration companies.

Large oil companies are a reasonably safe bet going forward because of several factors. First, as we discussed in an earlier chapter, they are extremely rich and they can always count on their political connections to bail them out if the going gets tough. With their huge war chests of cash, major oil companies are not limited to investing only in their own industry; they can always put their capital to work where it will make the most money. Second, oil is their product. When prices go higher, they make more money. Finally, most major oil companies pay handsome stock dividends, providing the investor with income as well as the potential for capital gains.

The four major oil companies are Exxon Mobile, ChevronTexaco, Royal Dutch Petroleum, and British Petroleum. While not fully appreciated, each major oil company is actually two companies in one. One part of the company explores for oil and produces it. When oil prices rise, that part of the company makes a lot of money. However, what about when oil prices fall? Even then, major oil companies make money because the other part of their company owns refineries. When oil prices decline, the operating profits rise for that part of the company because their costs for raw materials go down. Consequently, major oil companies make a lot of money when oil prices are rising and are still reasonably profitable in a declining price environment.

Another company that could benefit from both higher energy prices and China's growth is PetroChina. PetroChina is China's largest oil and natural gas producer. A secondary benefit to buying shares in PetroChina is that, if inflation continues to rise in the United States, the dollar will continue to depreciate against China's currency. Eventually, if China decides to allow their currency to float against the dollar, the stock will be revalued upward in dollars. If you decided to invest, you would find yourself in good company with the likes of Warren Buffett, who made a sizable investment in the company in 2003. You will find PetroChina's ADRs (American depository receipts) listed on the New York stock exchange.

Oil service companies' stock prices are far more volatile than the majors are, and therefore more risky. This sector can be broken down into diversified service companies and drillers. The most profitable and dominant diversified service company in the world is Schlumberger (SLB). It uses its technology to help the majors squeeze the most oil out of every well. Its services include geological analysis, drilling services, and well management. Halliburton (HAL) is another major oil service company. Generally, when oil has been in a bull market, the stock price of each of these companies has benefited.

Drillers build drilling rigs and lease them to major oil companies.

Table 6.3 Major Oil Companies

Exxon Mobile	XOM
Chevron Texaco	CVX
Royal Dutch Petroleum	RD
British Petroleum	BP
PetroChina	PRT

Table 6.4 Oil-Related Companies

Schlumberger	SLB	Diversified oil service company
Halliburton	HAL	Diversified oil service company
Nabors	NBR	Driller
Noble	NBL	Driller
Devon Energy	DVN	Independent exploration company

Unless oil companies find more oil, their businesses will eventually decline. Therefore, drillers should continue to benefit from exploration around the world. Two of the best companies in the field are Nabors (NBR), the world's largest land driller, and Noble (NBL).

Exploration companies, sometimes called independents, do just what the majors do: look for oil. Being smaller, they are more speculative. On the other hand, a major oil or natural gas strike by an independent will boost their stock price much more than it would for a major. One of the biggest and most successful of the independents is Devon Energy (DVN), whose annual revenues have grown to over seven billion dollars. The company has sizable in-the-ground reserves of both oil and natural gas, so rising prices of either will send this stock higher. One of Devon Energy's technological advantages is its expertise in horizontal drilling that has allowed it to boost production from marginal fields.

Rather than buying individual stocks, you may wish to invest in an energy mutual fund. Table 6.5 contains three to consider.

In additional to buying a managed mutual fund, you can also buy ETFs. Table 6.6 contains three to consider.

Table 6.5 Energy Mutual Funds

Vanguard Energy Fund	VDE	Diversified in major oil companies, oil service companies, and drillers
ICON Energy Fund	ICENX	Aggressive energy fund
Excelsior Energy Fund	UMESX	Hybrid fund invests in both energy and natural resources

Table 6.6 Energy ETFs

Energy Select Sector SPDR	XLE	Exposure to crude oil, natural gas, drilling, and other energy-related services
iShares Global Energy Sector Index Fund	IXC	Exposure to a wider selection of stocks of foreign companies
HOLDRs Oil Service Fund	OIH	Exposure to the oil service industry

In summary, there is an array of investment vehicles to choose from when you consider investing in energy. Table 6.7 will help you determine your best approach.

Your Plan of Attack

One of the primary indicators that you will want to monitor to alert you to imminent inflation is the price of commodities (major inputs of production). Just as stock market indexes tell you which way stock prices are heading, the Commodity Research Bureau Index (CRB) tells you if the prices of commodities (major inputs of production) are heading up or down. The CRB Index, which began trading on the New York Stock Futures Exchange in 1986, is the oldest of all commodity indexes. It consists of seventeen components that are equally weighted. Critics complain about this aspect of its construction. Equal weighting of the components gives the same weight to orange juice as to crude oil, which has fifty times the economic significance. Even so, the CRB is widely followed. You can monitor this index by going to http://futures.tradingcharts.com. There you will find free charts of, not only the CRB, but also all commodity and futures markets.

Table 6.7 Energy Investment Risk

Energy mutual funds	Least risk
Energy ETFs	Low risk
Energy stocks	Medium risk
Energy futures	High risk

Goldman Sachs created another exchange-traded index, the Goldman Sachs Commodity Index (GSCI), in 1992. Oil plays a much larger role in this index, often representing about one-half of the index, depending on the current price of oil. In 1999, Dow Jones created an index called the Dow Jones-AIG Commodity Index. Liquidity and worldwide production are the factors that determine the weighting of individual components.

Jim Rogers developed the Rogers Raw Materials Index in 1998, in an attempt to overcome some of the construction anomalies of the CRB and GSCI. Consisting of thirty-five commodities, this is the broadest and most comprehensive of the indexes. The importance in international commerce determines each component's importance and their weightings have been pre-fixed. You can find this index and its monthly performance since 1998 on the web at http://www.rogersrawmaterials.com.

In addition to developing and managing the Rogers Raw Materials Index, Jim Rogers is a highly respected and extremely successful international money manager who believes that we have recently begun a bull market in commodities that will last eighteen years, and not peak until sometime between 2013 and 2018. During that period, he also expects bonds to decline in value. If he is right, the next ten to fifteen years could resemble the 1970s. How do you take advantage of the expected rise in commodity prices? There are several ways.

1. *Invest in countries that are rich in natural resources.*

    In the coming years, their wealth will grow and their currencies will likely rise in value relative to the dollar. Moreover, their economies will prosper and their stock markets are likely to out-perform those in countries who must spend their currency in order to buy much-needed natural resources and commodities. The two countries poised to benefit most from the commodities boom are Canada and Australia. Both are home to a wealth of natural resources and have some of the largest mines in the world. To buy the entire country's stock market, you can again use ETFs. IShares offers an Australia Fund (EWA) and a Canada Fund (EWC). Other countries that may benefit from a rise in natural resource prices are New Zealand, Brazil, and Chile. New Zealand is a smaller version of Australia; Brazil is the largest producer of sugar, and Chile is the leading exporter of copper.

2. *Open a futures trading account and buy a contract on a commodity index.*
   Buy either one Goldman Sachs Commodity Index futures contract or one Commodity Research Bureau's Index futures contract.

3. *Buy stocks of commodity companies.*
   Two commodity companies I like are Bunge (BG), a global agribusiness company, and BHP Billiton (BHP), the world's largest natural resource company. I will go into more detail regarding this company in the next chapter.

4. *Buy a commodity mutual fund.*
   Two commodity mutual funds with good records are PIMCO's Commodity Real Return Strategy Fund (PCRAX), which seeks to match the return of the Dow Jones-AIG Commodity Index, and the Oppenheimer Real Asset Fund (QRAAX), which attempts to match the Goldman Sachs Commodity Index.

5. *Invest in a commodity futures fund.*
   Professional futures traders should do very well in this coming cycle because it is much easier to make money in bull markets than in bear markets or in markets that are range-bound for years.

To learn more about commodity futures funds, you can go to Managed Accounts Reports, whose business it is to monitor and track commodity trading advisors (CTAs) and commodity funds. They offer a fifty-two-page study entitled, "The Role of Managed Futures in Investment Portfolios" for a nominal fee. Their address is 200 Fifth Avenue, New York, NY 10001. MAR's research shows that when portfolios add a managed futures component to the mix, the risk/reward ratio improves. The ideal managed futures component for a bond portfolio is 9 percent; for a stock and bond portfolio, 14 percent is the ideal mix.

A word of caution: if you speak with a commodity broker, he may offer to manage your account. In general, I would advise against that. Unlike a CTA, who must make money for you in order to stay in business, a commodity broker makes his living from commissions. The more trades he places on your behalf, the more money he makes. Therefore, the potential for overtrading ("churning") your account exists. Furthermore, if the broker were an exceptionally good trader, he would become a CTA and manage money, which is much more lucrative. A broker, however, is sometimes a good place to start to find a good CTA.

Another way to learn more about commodities is to subscribe to either *Futures* magazine or *Stocks and Commodities* magazine. Over the years, I have contributed research articles to both of these magazines. In every issue, you can find good articles geared to the beginning commodity trader. Barnes and Noble carries both of these publications so you might be able to browse through an issue at your local bookstore. Otherwise, see www.futuresmag.com and www.traders.com.

7

How to Profit from the Race for Resources

I believe that banking institutions are more dangerous to our liberties than standing armies. If the American people ever allow private banks to control the issue of their currency, first by inflation, then by deflation, the banks and corporations that will grow up around [the banks] will deprive the people of all property until their children wake-up homeless on the continent their fathers conquered...[1]

~ Thomas Jefferson

The United States is potentially facing an inflationary crisis of unknown proportions brought about by excessive credit creation, which promotes an artificial expansion of the money supply. The more money that the government creates, either overtly by printing money or by the more subtle method of credit creation, the more it lowers the value of dollars already in existence.

Just Thinking about Inflation Can Cause Inflation

In a fiscally responsible world, one party deposits his savings in a bank. A second party then borrows the money, paying interest for the privilege of using that money now. The first party has delayed his gratification, while the second party has paid a price for instant gratification. Inflation disrupts that process.

To illustrate, assume that your roof needs replacing and it will cost $10,000. You have only $5,000, but you hope to save another $5,000 over the course of the year so that you will be ready to put on your new roof next year. Then you learn that roofing costs are increasing so quickly that by the time you have saved enough to pay for the roof, it will cost between $12,000 and $14,000. Instead of leaving your $5,000 in the bank and adding to it over the course of the coming year, you may now decide to take your $5,000 out of the bank and borrow an additional $5,000 to complete your roof before prices go higher.

From this example, you can see how inflationary expectations can distort a market. As people realize that important things will cost more in the future, they borrow money to secure those things now. Excess credit and a limited supply of desirable objects — such as prime real estate — combine to cause artificial demand and a bubble environment. While the government tells us that inflation is contained because CPI numbers are low, in fact, asset inflation is very much alive. Moreover, asset inflation decreases savings, which are needed to grow the economy.

The current environment is not unlike the mid-1970s when the country underwent an invisible crash. It was invisible because, on the surface, it appeared that Americans had more money than ever. However, after adjusting for inflation, Americans' real wealth was declining. Higher inflation rates begot higher interest rates, leading to a decrease in the value on bonds, which represented a large portion of Americans' wealth.

A Dozen Ways to Buy Gold

There are several extremely good reasons why gold should play a role in our monetary system. Unlike paper currency, gold is indestructible; the supply of gold does not change much over time and it is portable. Governments cannot easily manipulate gold. On a gold standard, the quantity of money could only increase in relation to the quantity of gold.

We cannot guess what role, if any, gold will play in the future monetary affairs of men. All we can really know is that the supply of gold is relatively fixed. At today's prices, all the gold in the world is only worth about a half trillion dollars. Analysts predict that the gold price would need to rise to between $3,000 and $5,000 an ounce before being fairly valued. On the other hand, other analysts point out that after gold reached record highs in the 1970s, increased exploration brought more gold to market every year for the next two decades. As inflation declined in the 1980s and 1990s, the demand for gold lessened. The growing supply and falling demand sent gold into a long bear market.

Unlike some of the other commodities we have examined, gold inventories are now the highest they have been in years. Furthermore, because it is indestructible, we cannot use it up. All the gold ever mined is still with us. Meanwhile, about half of all the world's mining companies are involved in gold mining. Newmont Mining, the world's largest gold-mining company, has been producing a surplus and sees production increasing for at least the next few years. Another psychological negative is that, at this time, most of the world's central banks have little interest in holding gold and often use rallies to unload some of their reserves. China's central bank is the only exception.

Gold has many industrial uses, but any rise in price will likely result from speculative activity, which could come from overseas. Recently, the Chinese government, for the first time in decades, has allowed its citizens to own gold. Given that gold has a long history as a savings vehicle in China, the new policy might one day prove to be very bullish for the market. Remember that, because China's economy is growing so quickly, the Chinese are at risk for inflation as well. They can now protect themselves from inflation by purchasing gold on the Shanghai Gold

Exchange. Meanwhile, in America, a new ETF that allows direct owner-ship of gold through a fund began trading. The new ETF makes it very easy for speculators, money managers, and even institutions to own gold.

Given the fact that the market cap for tradable gold and silver is less than 100 billion dollars, if the investment community channels even a tiny fraction of their assets into gold, we could see a sharp price rise. If inflation begins to rise and investors return to gold as an inflation hedge, the price will certainly increase. Once price increases make the headlines, other investors will pile in. Sentiment will play a major part in any gold move, and sentiment is difficult to predict. However, you probably will not go wrong by making a small investment in gold, and you might want to monitor the market to be ready to invest more as you see signs that a bull market is underway. How can you invest? Here are three ways:

1. Buy gold stocks.
2. Buy gold funds.
3. Buy gold ETFs.

Here are my favorite gold stocks.

- *Gold Pick #1*

  Newmont Mining (NEM) is the world's largest gold producer. According to the company, each $10 rise in the price of gold trans-lates into $58 million in profits for the company. While many gold mining companies hedge their production (meaning that they sell their future production ahead at a fixed price), Newmont does not. What that means is that its profits increase more dramatically when the price of gold rises. Moreover, Newmont has state-of-the art mining technology. In 1997, it opened the largest research lab built by a mining company in over twenty-five years.

  Newmont has other mining interests as well. The growing automobile industry in China will create demand for just about anything that is used in automobiles. Magnesium, which is 75 per-cent lighter than steel, is seeing increasing demand for engine blocks. Newmont owns a major interest in the Australian Magne-sium Corporation, which is likely to become the largest supplier of magnesium to the automotive industry. In summary, Newmont's technology combined with its position as the world's largest gold-mining company, should allow its stock price to benefit handsomely from rising gold prices.

- *Gold Pick #2*
AngloGold (AU) is the world's second largest gold producer with operations in eight different countries. Unlike Newmont, Anglo-Gold does hedge its production. However, given that it produces nearly six million ounces a year, its stock should still benefit greatly from any rise in the price of gold. This company is also actively engaged in research for new applications for gold. One avenue that looks promising is the use of gold in catalytic converters. Currently, these emission control devices use platinum and rhodium, both of which are much more expensive than gold at present prices. It is also exploring the possibility of using gold in fuel cells.

 AngloGold is a South African company so you will need to buy their stock through ADRs (American depository receipts), which trade just like any other stock. Given the company's attention to research and marketing, as well as its hefty production, AngloGold should not disappoint if gold prices rise.

- *Gold Pick #3*
Barrick Gold (ABX), a Canadian company, is the world's third largest producer with operations in North and South America as well as Australia. Barrick has probable reserves of 86 million ounces and plenty of cash, which could mean future acquisitions of smaller gold mining companies. Barrick has traditionally hedged their forward production, and the company is preparing to take advantage of potentially higher gold prices by unwinding their hedges.

- *Gold Pick #4*
GoldCorp (GG) is another outstanding Canadian gold-mining company worth investigating. Not only is the company unhedged, but it keeps its entire cash reserves in gold as well. This company's

strong balance sheet also puts it in a position to acquire smaller companies.

- *Gold Pick #5*

  Placer Dome (PDG) is the fifth largest producer in the world with proven reserves of 50 million ounces. In addition, it owns several large properties where they might make future discoveries. It also has a strong cash position.

- *Gold Pick #6*

  Harmony Gold (HMY) is another major unhedged gold miner located in South Africa. One of its advantages is that it owns its own refinery and fabrication plants. It also sells gold bars and jewelry directly from its website, www.harmonygold-direct.com.

The following tables will give you six major gold stocks, three major gold funds, and two gold ETFs to consider.

It makes sense to keep a portion of your assets in gold if for no other reason than for insurance against an uncertain economic future. With all the different investment vehicles at your disposal, you can be as conservative or as aggressive as you care to be.

If you would like to invest in gold, take some time to educate yourself further on the subject. There is no shortage of information about the gold market. A good place to start is the World Gold Council's website (www.gold.org). The World Gold Council consists of mining companies from all over the world that want to promote gold's advantages. On the site, you will find the latest industry news, statistics, and forecasts along with a number of interesting articles. You may also want to visit www.kitco.com, another free site that offers historical charts, market commentary, and a wealth of articles written by market advisors.

Five Reasons to be a Silver Bull

Unlike gold, silver has been primarily used and priced as an industrial metal. Forty percent of all silver usage is for industrial applications. Jew-

Table 7.1 Gold Stocks

Newmont Mining	NEM	World's largest producer
Anglogold	AU	Partially hedged
Barrick Gold	ABX	Cash-rich Canadian miner
GoldCorp	GG	Cash reserves in gold
Placer Dome	PDG	Strong cash position
Harmony Gold	HMY	South African miner and refiner

Table 7.2 Gold Funds

ASA Ltd.	ASA	Invests in gold-mining companies, mostly in South Africa.
Tocqueville Gold Fund	TGLDX	Invests 65 percent of its fund's money in gold-mining shares.
Precious Metals UltraSector ProFund	PMPIX	Leveraged to 150% of Dow Jones Precious Metals Index.

Table 7.3 Gold ETFs

Gold Miner's Index	GDM	36 gold- and silver-mining companies
StreetTracks Gold Trust	GLD	Shares represent actual gold

Table 7.4 Gold Investor's Risk

ETFs	Low risk
Gold Funds	Low risk
Gold Stocks	Medium risk
Gold Futures	High risk

elry accounts for another 30 percent of usage and photography accounts for 20 percent. Thus, during good economic times, there is more demand for silver and the price tends to rise. Conversely, when the economy slows, demand for silver also slows and its price declines. We saw that occur during the 1990s. With the strong economy and an explosion in technology, the demand for silver was strong and the price of silver rose accordingly. During that same period, the price of gold declined. After the stock market peaked in 2000 and the economy slowed, the price of silver retreated while gold's price moved higher. Today, there are five good reasons to be a silver bull.

1. Unlike the effect of price on most commodities, higher silver prices will not affect demand because silver's applications in industrial processes represent only a tiny fraction of the final product. Moreover, wherever silver is used in industry, there is generally no substitute.

2. Because the dollar value of the silver market is relatively small compared to gold or most other investment markets, even a small increase in demand would cause prices to rise dramatically.

3. Current demand for fabrication at 800 million ounces a year is outpacing annual production of 600 million ounces a year.

4. There are not many primary silver mines. Most silver comes as a by-product of lead-zinc mines, gold mines, or copper mines.

5. Of all the metals, there is less silver remaining underground relative to current usage.

The last factor may be the most important. Like oil, the supply of metals underground is finite. Unlike oil, however, most silver deposits lie near the surface. Therefore, digging deeper will not help. According to the United States Geological Survey, at present usage rates, we could deplete all proven reserves of silver in fourteen years. Even if we take unproven reserves into account, the supply of silver will only last twenty-nine years. To put that in perspective, remember that mankind has mined and used silver for five thousand years. This geological data strongly suggests that within our lifetimes, there will be no more silver available at any price.

Whenever I read about projected demand, I consider what hidden demand could emerge. In the case of silver, I am quite certain that government estimates of usage do not adequately account for China's industrial growth. If that is the case, we could run out of known reserves much sooner. As is the case with oil, the supply does not have to completely

Table 7.5 Silver-Mining Companies

Apex Silver	SIL	George Soros is an investor
Pan American Silver	PAAS	Bill Gates is an investor
Hecla	HL	Produces 8.7 million ounces annually
Silver Standard	SSO-CDNX	Highly leveraged to silver price increases

run out to cause sharp price increases. Instead, the market must simply realize that supplies will run out at some time in the not too distant future. When that occurs, hording begins to take place by companies who will eventually require the resource. Farsighted investors will do the same.

Quite possibly, we may be beginning to see the tip of that iceberg. Warren Buffet, the legendary investment wizard, recently bought large amounts of silver bullion. Additionally, George Soros, one of the world's richest investors and hedge fund managers, bought shares in Apex Silver (SIL). Closer to home, Bill Gates now owns 13.7 percent of Pan American Silver (PAAS).

Two other major silver-mining companies worth your investigation are Hecla (HL) and Silver Standard (SSO-CDNX), which trades on the Toronto Stock Exchange. Hecla operates three large mines that produce both gold and silver. In all, it produces 8.7 million ounces of silver annually and expects to double its gold production over the next five years.

Silver Standard controls the world's largest published in-ground silver resources, with a portfolio of core properties in Argentina, Mexico, Chile, Peru, the United States, and Australia. The company's strategy is to acquire high-quality, diverse silver projects with defined resources in anticipation of higher silver prices. The company purchased or optioned all of its projects at a fraction of the current price of silver. Thus, Silver Standard shares offer investors high leverage to silver price increases.

China Needs These Metals

Base metals include nickel, copper, aluminum, steel, palladium, and many others. Nearly every manufactured item contains traces of these metals. Because the economy drives the market for base metals, the market is cyclical. However, when thinking about demand for base metals, you must think outside of the American market. China's demand for base metals will soon surpass ours. It will require an inordinate amount of steel and copper to build factories and apartment buildings to house the tens of millions of peasants that are flocking to the major cities.

The demand for automobiles, as you know, is exploding in China. More than 100 million Chinese are ready to cross the income threshold that will allow them to afford to buy their first car. That is why all the major automobile manufacturers, including such giants as GM, Ford, Daimler-Chrysler, Fiat, BMW, Toyota, and Honda, have built assembly operations in China. In another interesting turn of events, China has developed an auto-parts manufacturing industry in anticipation of the millions of cars that will soon be on China's highways. China is now a major exporter of auto parts and will soon be competing in a big way with Western manufacturers for base metals to build their cars, trucks, buses, railroads, and airplanes, as well as to fuel their growing automotive parts industry. It does not take a genius to figure out that demand for base metals is about to explode.

Base metals are cyclical commodities. When prices are low, there is little incentive to invest hundreds of millions of dollars in new exploration projects. Mining companies cut back on exploration and stay in business by keeping costs down and continuing to work the old mines. Eventually, however, mines wear out and companies halt production. With less metal brought to market, even relatively stable demand can sometimes tip the balance in favor of suppliers, causing prices to rise.

As prices rise, mining companies bring in more cash and begin to think about exploration again. However, prices need to rise a lot before mining companies will commit to spending hundreds of millions of dollars on a new mine.

In the case of nickel, it appears that new supplies are simply not going to arrive in time to meet the rising worldwide demand for the metal. That means that the bull market in nickel could last a long time. While you can buy nickel on the London Metal Exchange, you may also want to consider playing the nickel market by purchasing shares in either Inco

(N) or Falconbridge Ltd. (FAL), two of the world's largest producers. Learn more about these companies at www.inco.com and www.falcon-bridge.com.

Unlike nickel, copper inventories are relatively high, but strong demand could cause a depletion of supplies at some time in the future. While copper could lag some of the other base metals, you might benefit from having more time to invest. The copper industry has undergone a great deal of consolidation, and new, more efficient technologies have allowed the remaining large copper companies to make a good profit. Phelps Dodge (PD) is one of the world's premier copper companies and deserves monitoring, along with the price of copper. Other major copper companies include Freeport McMoran (FCX) and Lumina Copper (LCC).

China's growth will lead to more demand for steel and aluminum. Two well-positioned steel companies, U.S. Steel (X) and Nucor (NUE) could benefit. Meanwhile, higher aluminum prices would benefit Alcoa (AA).

The World's Most Despised Metal

The first warning came from the Roman architect, Vitruvius, who claimed that lead was harmful to the human system. He believed that Romans were getting sick from the water that ran through lead pipes. In spite of his warnings, for the next two centuries, lead found many uses. In medieval times, Europeans used it in their cathedrals. Americans later found uses for lead in bullets, pipes, paints, solders, gasoline, and batteries. By the 1980s, however, lead's reputation began to tarnish. Small children were dying from lead poisoning – most likely after amusing themselves by eating chips of lead-based paint when no one was looking. The government stepped in and banned lead from paint, solders, and gasoline.

Barraged with lawsuits, the once prosperous lead industry found itself fighting for survival. After being in business for eighty-four years, the Lead Industries Association, Inc., filed for bankruptcy in 1982. Lead's popularity continued to wane. Lead poisoning was turning up just about everywhere lead could be found — especially in towns near smelters and mines.

Lead's image and prospects for growth are no better outside the United States. Reports of lead poisoning have surfaced in towns near mines and smelters in Peru and Africa. In Australia, hundreds of people living near lead smelters have filed lawsuits. Meanwhile, in the United States, the federal government recently relocated more than one hundred families living near a smelter in Herculaneum, Missouri, due to lead poisoning. The evidence is rather convincing that environmental concerns would thwart any attempt to mine lead or build a new lead smelter anywhere in the world. Lead production is in decline and that trend should continue. We now need to look at what the demand for lead will be going forward.

Lead is rapidly disappearing from many products. With the exception of road paints, governments have outlawed lead based paints. Lead used in gasoline additives has met the same fate. These trends are not limited to the United States; phase-outs are in effect throughout the world.

However, TVs and computer monitors still require lead. So do ammunitions, telecommunications, glass, roofing, and X-ray machines. As the rest of the world industrializes, you can expect increased demand for all of these products. Moreover, demand is growing rapidly for lead's primary product, lead-acid storage batteries used primarily in cars and trucks. While it is true that newer batteries last longer, which could cause the demand for replacement batteries in the United States and Europe to decline slightly in coming years, the demand from China, India, and South America is exploding and should more than offset the decline in demand from the West. Every new vehicle that takes to the road in these countries will require a battery, and every battery will require lead.

Where will the industry get the additional lead with supplies declining? It will buy it on the open market – at the London Metal Exchange, where producers and processors have traded lead since 1903. For information on how you can buy lead, contact the London Metals Exchange at www.lme.co.uk. Incidentally, the largest lead mine in the world is the Cannington mine in Queensland, Australia. The owner and operator is BHP Billiton, one of the world's largest mining companies and one of my favorite natural resource companies.

The Big Dog in Natural Resources

In the field of natural resources, BHP Billiton does it all. BHP is the fourth largest producer of aluminum, the third largest producer of copper, and a leading supplier of lead and zinc. It also supplies core raw materials and services to the international steel industry. Finally, it produces 4 percent of the world's diamonds.

BHP is also one of the world's largest producers of coal, servicing the major power markets of Europe, Asia, and the United States In addition, it also runs a significant oil and gas business, with producing operations in Australia, the United Kingdom, the Gulf of Mexico, Pakistan, and Algeria. Finally, BHP is the world's fourth largest nickel producer. Because of all these businesses, BHP Billiton is the largest natural resource company in the world.

Another strong positive for the company is its ideal location. Based in Australia, it is uniquely situated to serve the growing demands for natural resources from China and Southeast Asia. An investment in BHP Billiton is a logical way to benefit from rising commodity prices and higher inflation.

The Next Big Thing

Over four hundred nuclear power plants span the globe, producing 20 percent of the world's electricity. Because the world is running out of oil, and coal is environmentally unfriendly, nuclear reactors have become the top choice to bridge the half-century gap between fossil fuels and some new alternative energy source.

In fact, one of the most outspoken advocates of nuclear energy is the internationally renowned environmentalist Dr. James Lovelock, who achieved fame through his publication of the Gaia hypothesis, which makes the case that the earth keeps itself fit for life by the actions of living things themselves. To his credit, Lovelock was among the first to warn of global warming.

Dr. Lovelock claims that there is simply not enough time for renewable energy, such as wind and solar power — the favored solutions of the Green movement — to take the place of the coal, gas, and oil-fired power stations whose carbon dioxide is causing the atmosphere to warm. He believes that only a massive expansion of nuclear power, which produces almost no carbon dioxide, can now check a runaway warming that may raise sea levels disastrously around the world, cause climatic turbulence, and make agriculture unviable over large areas.[2]

The world seems to agree. According to the World Nuclear Association, thirty new nuclear plants are currently under construction throughout the world, with eighteen in Southeast Asia. China, India, and South Korea all have big nuclear construction programs. As these countries and countries in South America continue to industrialize, the demand for electricity will continue to grow. That demand will certainly be met to some degree by nuclear power.

In the United States, the administration has made the construction of new nuclear energy plants a top priority. In 2003, when Bush outlined a new energy policy in his State of the Union address, the bulk of the money, some $15 billion, was earmarked to pay for a new generation of nuclear power plants. The money would provide for six or seven large new plants. While that is a good first step, the Nuclear Regulatory Commission believes that, because of increasing demand, we will require as many as one hundred new plants.

The Senate Conference Committee also vowed to include loan guarantees of up to 50 percent of costs for the construction of new nuclear plants, and guaranteed that the government would purchase power from those plants at a premium price. The bill also earmarked over one billion dollars for a demonstration plant that would use nuclear energy to create hydrogen, which could be used to fuel cars. Advocates say that nuclear power will help reduce the country's dependence on foreign oil and give America the lead in energy technology. They also argue that it solves the problem of pollution caused by fossil fuels and offers the best defense against global warming.

The goal would be to increase worldwide capacity by three to five times. If that occurred, experts believe that far more uranium would be required than we have known reserves. It is important to remember that, unlike other commodities, there is no substitute for uranium. Once the plants are built, they must have uranium or they will not be able to operate. In short, uranium companies will need to find uranium somewhere and pay whatever it costs or watch the lights go out in an entire region.

There is no doubt that for the next half-century we will see strong growth in the demand for electricity, most notably in China. To meet that demand, China, Japan, and other countries throughout the world will build new nuclear power plants as quickly as possible. In fact, China recently announced that it plans to build as many as thirty new nuclear plants by 2020. Even then, China would only be able to meet three percent of its energy needs. Unless China continues to burn coal, it will need hundreds more. Meanwhile, Japan — a country completely dependent on other countries for its energy needs — plans to build eleven more reactors by 2010.

The demand for uranium to power these plants will be great. An analysis of current production indicates that demand will far outweigh future supplies, resulting in a sharp increase in the price of uranium. Already, even before the new plants are finished, the demand for uranium is running well ahead of annual production and prices are rising.

Higher uranium prices will stimulate exploration. Nevertheless, even if a mining company is lucky enough to discover a uranium deposit, it takes five to ten years to bring the metal to market. Meanwhile, expect nuclear power plants to scramble for existing supplies, bidding prices ever higher.

Unfortunately, unlike lead, you cannot go out and buy uranium. There are only five hundred buyers in the world — utility companies that, once a week, meet with producers to negotiate contracts. You are not invited to the party. The next best idea is to look for companies that will profit from rising prices.

Canada's Athabasca Basin has produced some of the world's best mines. One company, Cameco (CCJ) sits on these deposits – possibly the highest-grade, lowest-cost deposits in the world. As a result, Cameco is the lowest-cost producer and dominates the world market for uranium. It has total reserves of 550 million pounds and controls two of the world's largest, highest-grade, and long-life reserves. Cameco is also the only company with mines in the United States (Wyoming and Nebraska).

Cameco's operations also include gold mining, diamond exploration, and nuclear power plants.

Another company likely to benefit from higher uranium prices is Denison Mines (DEN.TO). Though a much smaller player than Cameco, Denison has an environmental division that specializes in cleaning up old uranium sites. Additionally, Denison is the only company in Canada, besides Cameco, that is actually producing uranium. Moreover, Denison has considerable proven ore reserves and is actively engaged in exploration on prime properties located in the Athabascan Basin. Energy Resources of Australia (EGRAF) is a third major player.

If you find that PE ratios for these three companies have become too exorbitant, you may want to investigate some of the exploration companies, remembering that mining-exploration companies are far more speculative. One worth looking at is International Uranium Company (IUC), which recently made an exciting new discovery in the Athabascan Basin. Like Denison, International Uranium is also engaged in extensive exploration.

What's Old Is New Again

While coal might seem outdated as an energy source, for most of the world it is a step forward. We must remember that many societies are just now entering the age of industrialization. Wealth per capita is growing quickly. As people get money, they buy refrigerators, washer/dryers, motorcycles, cars, and boats. As a result, they use more electricity. The entire planet will require more energy each year. Yet, we are running out of fossil fuels, and oil will continue to become more expensive. Where will we turn?

To answer that question, you need to know what is going on in China. Total energy demand is rising almost 15 percent every year. China accounts for two-thirds of the global growth in energy demand. In order to satisfy its growing demand, China expects to double its current rate of capacity growth. Where will the energy come from?

China leads the world in coal consumption. Last year, it used one-third of the world's production, while the United States consumed about

22 percent. China's coal imports have increased dramatically. Coal provides power for more than three-quarters of China's electrical power plants. Because China's electrical energy consumption will continue to increase, we can expect the demand for coal to rise significantly for many years to come.

The coal industry has seen its share of hard times. Because of environmental concerns, utilities stopped building any new coal-fired electrical plants decades ago. Many coal-mining companies, faced with health care and pension issues, went out of business. No one could have anticipated China's tremendous demand for coal today. Now, more than one hundred new coal-fired plants are on the drawing board.

Unlike some of the metals we have studied, there is no shortage of coal. The planet has enough coal to last hundreds of years. For the last two years, however, demand has outstripped supply. The result is that coal-mining companies are making money and their fortunes look bright – at least over the near term. Peabody Coal (BTU) dominates the center of the coal chessboard. An international player, Peabody also has strong ties to Washington. Another beneficiary of China's demand for steel will be the Fording Canadian Coal Trust (FDG). Fording is a major producer of coke, which is the type of coal used in steel plants.

Going forward, the wildcard for coal will be environmental issues. Coal burning is extremely carbon-dioxide intensive. On the other hand, China and India require cheap energy, and coal is their main source of fuel. It is unlikely that environmental factors will outweigh economic factors in these two countries.

The World's Most Expensive Rock

Diamonds result when molten rock heats and pressurizes carbon and then pushes it to the surface in volcanic pipes made of kimberlite. Not all kimberlite pipes contain diamonds, but the few that do make the search worthwhile. Rough diamonds are worth about $172,000 a pound. Compare that to gold, with a price per pound of only about $4,500. Moreover, the price of diamonds increases ten times over before reaching the retail jewelry market. Over the last fifteen years, a 250 percent increase in demand for diamonds from the jewelry sector has contributed to rising prices.

Some of the biggest diamond discoveries lately have come from Canada. Finding diamonds in Canada is good news for Canadian mining companies and Canada in general. When small-mining exploration companies discover diamonds, larger international companies often take them over. In order to buy the mines or companies, the foreign companies must first convert their currency to Canadian dollars, thus giving the Loonie a boost and adding wealth to the entire Canadian economy.

Two factors will increase the demand for diamonds. First, more Chinese men will achieve an income level sufficient to allow them to afford a small diamond ring for their loved one. Second, all over the world, the rich are getting richer and diamond rings are getting bigger, even on younger women. Furthermore, according to Charles Wyndham, co-founder of www International Diamond Consultants Ltd., their latest forecasts show demand for diamonds continuing to rise at least until 2012, based on projected GDP in all key markets.

While the cost to recover diamonds in Canada is high, their quality is excellent. One example is the popular polar bear diamonds produced by Sirius Diamonds Ltd. of Vancouver (www.siriusdiamonds.com). Furthermore, Canadian mines are not subject to the political uncertainties of Botswana or Russia. Retailers prefer doing business with Canadian companies because they know that civil wars and other political problems will not interrupt their supplies. Moreover, the diamond industry in other parts of the world continues to suffer from accusations of using slave labor and claims that military cartels have received some of the industry's mining proceeds.

A final reason to expect Canada to increase its share of the diamond industry is that production in other countries has been decreasing as the industry depletes mines faster than they make new discoveries. For all these reasons, demand for Canadian diamonds, which represents only 15 percent of the world market, should continue to grow. But how can you make money from this trend?

Without a doubt, some Canadian diamond-mining companies will make a fortune. One diamond mine can potentially produce as much as

$50 billion dollars over its lifetime. Unfortunately, it is impossible to know which ones will strike it rich. Investors faced the same situation concerning Internet companies in the early 1990s. One solution is to buy a few shares in several companies and hope that one will strike pay dirt.

BHP Billiton (BHP) and Aber Diamond Corporation (ABER) have already made discoveries and will reap huge profits once their mines go into operation. Other companies that are still digging away include Diamondex Resources Ltd., Ashton Mining of Canada Inc., Tahera Corporation, Majescor Resources, Stornoway Diamond Corporation, and Diamond North Resources Ltd. The best way to learn about these companies is to use the Internet, go to their websites, and do a little research. It might just be worth the effort.

Making Money from Plant Food

Not quite as glamorous as diamonds and gold, fertilizer is also a natural resource. Like its upscale cousins also found beneath the earth's crust, mining companies must dig fertilizer out and process it before it has value. At that point, fertilizer becomes to plants what vitamins are to humans. To stay healthy, plants need three "vitamins":

1. Nitrogen — Plants absorb nitrogen through their root systems. Urea is an example of a nitrogen fertilizer.
2. Phosphorous — Phosphorous comes from the mineral phosphate. Phosphate deposits are primarily found in Africa, China, Russia, and the United States.
3. Potassium — Potassium comes from potash. Canada leads the world in the production of potash, while Russia is second.

When global demand for food is high, farm commodities bring higher prices. With the extra profit, farmers plant more fields and the demand for fertilizer goes up. In turn, the price rises and companies that produce fertilizer profit.

The largest increase in agriculture is occurring in developing countries. As their economies grow, their agricultural industries will require more fertilizer. Does that mean that we should buy fertilizer companies? It depends what kind of fertilizer they make. Those companies that produce nitrogen fertilizers will not benefit as one would expect because China has banned urea imports and has become a net exporter of nitrogen-based fertilizers. Companies that produce phosphate fertilizers are now competing with aggressive companies in India and Australia, who have produced so much that inventories are high.

The story for the third plant vitamin, potassium, is different. Potassium is a compound made from potash. Unlike nitrogen-based fertilizers, China has no potash reserves. You will remember that nearly half of all potash production occurs in Canada. The world's largest producer of this plant vitamin is the Potash Corporation (POT), located in Saskatchewan. It owns the largest and lowest-cost reserve of potash in the world. Because of this, it has pricing control over the global market. When demand is strong for potash, it can easily produce more; when it is weak, it can produce less.

As the world's population continues to increase, demand for food will increase as well. It is important that farmers maximize the yield on their crops because the amount of available farmland is not keeping up with the demand for food. Therefore, I would expect the demand for fertilizers to increase in the future. Only one of the three types is absent in China, and one company controls that type of fertilizer. Because of that, as a final — if not glamorous resource play — you may consider the dominant company in the field, the Potash Corporation, worthy of further investigation.

Why Own Metals and Natural Resources?

While each metal, base or precious, has its own fundamentals and its own cycles, metals and natural resources have, as a group, begun an upswing that could last for some time. While dollars will depreciate in the decade ahead, the price of metals should go considerably higher, and thus act as a hedge against inflation. Here are some of the fundamentals that could drive demand.

- Gold: New investment vehicles have made ownership as easy as buying a stock. As inflation picks up, investors could panic into gold, sending the price much higher.

- Silver: Demand is already outstripping supply. Moreover, underground silver supplies are rapidly running out. Some of the smartest investors in the world have already taken positions.

- Base metals: Strong growth in China will continue to drive the demand for all base metals. Nickel could be a standout.

- Lead: Denigrated for more than two decades, the world will soon realize that it needs more lead for car batteries than it has. BHP Billiton could benefit.

- Uranium: An essential input for nuclear reactors, uranium supplies are limited and difficult to find. As more reactors come online, shortages could develop, sending prices much higher. Cameco, the world's leading producer, would profit.

- Coal: Still the cheapest energy source, developing countries will demand more coal, most likely ignoring environmental concerns. Peabody and Fording should benefit.

- Diamonds: As the rich get richer and world income levels rise, so will the demand for diamonds. Canada will benefit along with a handful of lucky diamond-mining companies.

- Fertilizer: Rarely considered in the natural resource area, potassium-based fertilizer should see increased demand from China and the rest of the world as food demand increases. The Potash Corporation is poised to exploit that demand.

Gold-mining stocks and silver stocks have appeared in previous tables. This table will help you find stocks that will benefit from rising prices in platinum, nickel, copper, steel, lead, uranium, coal, diamonds, and fertilizer.

In this chapter, you learned how to protect yourself from inflation by investing in natural resources. In the next chapter, you will learn how to hedge (insure against a drop in value) any financial assets you may own by purchasing special types of CDs. In addition, you will learn why you should not lend money (note: buying a bond is the same as lending money) and six ways to protect yourself against rising interest rates.

Table 7.6 Mining Stocks

INCO	N	Nickel	One of world's largest producers
Falconbridge Ltd.	FAL	Nickel	One of world's largest producers
Phelps Dodge	PD	Copper	Premier company
Freeport McMoran	FCX	Copper	Major producer
Lumina Copper	LCC	Copper	Major producer
U.S. Steel	X	Steel	Major producer
Nucor	NUE	Steel	Major producer
BHP Billiton	BHP	Various	Natural resource play
Cameco	CCJ	Uranium	High-grade, low-cost deposits
Denison Mines	DENMIF	Uranium	Proven reserves
Energy Resources of Australia	EGRAF	Uranium	Proven reserves
International Uranium Co.	IUC	Uranium	Not in production yet
Peabody	BTU	Coal	Dominates the industry
Fording Canadian Coal Trust	FDG	Coal	Produces coke for steel
Aber Diamond Corp.	ABER	Diamonds	Recent large discoveries
Potash Corp.	POT	Fertilizer	Largest potassium producer

FEDERAL RESERVE NOTE
THE UNITED STATES OF AMERICA
K 34478182 C
K 34478182 C
ONE DOLLAR

8

How to Protect Your Savings from Inflation

In the absence of the gold standard, there is no way to protect savings from confiscation through inflation. There is no safe store of value.[1]

~ Alan Greenspan

Historically, banks did not go out of their way to lend you money. Lately, that is not the case. Today, bankers rush to stuff money in your pocket as you are walking out the door. In fact, if you own a home, someone wants to lend you money. How did you get so lucky?

Banks and other financial institutions are eager to lend you money these days because they no longer incur the same risks that they did in the past. Now, they package their loans and sell them to someone else. Those people then repackage the loans and sell them to investors – pension funds, investment companies, and foreign investors. Debt is like a hot potato. The faster that banks can get a loan off their books, the faster they can make another loan. While it appears that everyone wins, one of the first laws of economics is that there is no such thing as a free lunch. Somebody must pay for lunch.

Who Pays for Lunch?

An economic truism is that there is no such thing as a free lunch — that is, someone must eventually pay. Yet the government acts as though lunch is there for the taking. The federal debt continues to grow, despite rhetoric from the administration about reducing the deficit. In addition, the trade deficit continues to widen. Each month we buy more from foreign countries than we produce and sell to them. Consequently, our dollars wind up in Asian banks. Those countries become richer, while we go further in debt. After accumulating our dollars through foreign trade, Asia reinvests them by purchasing our debt, which we issue each year in the form of government bonds. It is only the willingness of Japan and China to buy our government bonds that has allowed our government to continue to spend money.

We might say that, so far, Japan and China have been willing to buy our lunch. We Americans are a lucky bunch. As discussed earlier, part of our good fortune lies in the fact that the dollar is the de facto reserve currency of the world. That gives us the privilege to print as many dollars as we want and use them to buy real stuff from other countries. Other countries, however, are not fools. Just in the last few years, because of the depreciation of the dollar, Asian investors have lost almost a third of the money that they invested in our government debt. As a result, they are beginning to look for other places to put their money.

Over time, the dollar will continue to depreciate because the government continues to increase the money supply. We are not fully seeing the effect of that yet because we export so much money overseas. With the exception of the money that inflated the real estate bubble, we have exported much of our inflation. However, the world economy is a closed loop. We print money and send it east in return for finished products and credit that come west. Asia takes our dollars and lends them back to us.

So far, Japan and China have had little choice. It is not that they think our government bonds are such great investments. They send our money back to us because if they converted those dollars to their own currencies, the value of their currencies would rise against the value of the dollar, making their exports less competitive. It would seem that the highly productive Asian economies have their hands tied. However, that is not the case; they do have other alternatives. Instead of buying U.S debt, which becomes worth less as the dollar depreciates, China has recently begun buying productive tangible assets both in America and throughout the world. China is now using our dollars to buy natural resource companies that will benefit from America's inflation and the declining dollar.

If China decides to use their excess dollars to buy some of our productive industry or domestic natural resources, those dollars that we sent them will come back into our economy. The inflation that we so conveniently exported to them will come right back to us — that is, the chickens will come home to roost. Moreover, if Asians become less willing to buy our debt, the Federal Reserve will need to print even more money in order to pay its debts. Asia is not the one with the problem. The U.S. government, because of bad policy decisions, is the one that could find itself in an uncomfortable situation.

The Big Mac Theory

Why does the value of one currency rise against another and vice versa? One axiom is that money goes where it is treated best. What that means is that, all other things being equal, capital will flow to where interest rates are highest. For example, if your local bank will only pay you 3 percent interest on a one-year CD, but a bank in Australia will pay you 5 percent, it would make sense to send your money to Australia. Because Australia's higher interest rates would attract investment capital from around the world, the value of the currency would rise as well. That occurs because, an American, for example, would have to sell his U.S. dollars and buy Australian dollars before he could make the investment. More demand for Australian dollars drives the currency higher.

Following the same logic, if the United States wanted to attract foreign capital, the Federal Reserve could raise its interest rates significantly.

Capital would flow into the country and the U.S. dollar would strengthen. On the other hand, higher interest rates would hurt the economy. That is why the Federal Reserve would be reluctant to take such measures. Every central bank must balance the effects of a strong versus a weak currency. In general, higher interest rates promote a stronger currency, which, in turn, hurts manufacturers who export abroad because their products become more costly to foreigners. Higher interest rates also hurt employment and the stock market. In conclusion, raising interest rates to boost the value of the currency is usually not a good idea. Instead, it is wiser to build a strong economy, which will attract foreign investment to the stock market.

It sounds as though you should simply send your money to where the highest interest rates prevail. Unfortunately, it is not that easy. Sometimes, countries raise their interest rates to combat inflation. In that case, while you might earn a good rate of interest in a particular country, inflation could erase your gains. There are many banana republics in third world countries that offer very high rates of interest, but often those countries are in crisis. Remember, you will need to convert your U.S. dollars to their currency before you can take advantage of their high interest rates. Depending on the country, you could also incur political risk (because of an unstable government), which might lead to currency devaluation.

Currencies of resource-rich countries like Australia and Canada are likely to move higher as China continues to invest money in natural resources and the companies that own them. Remember, money flowing into a country is a prescription for an overheated economy and inflation. Higher interest rates act to slow borrowing and keep the economy from overheating. As you can see, the crosscurrents in global currency valuations are rather complex. Sometimes, you just have to figure out where you can get a Big Mac at a reasonable price.

No, I am not being facetious. The *Economist* magazine publishes a Big Mac Index. The theory behind the index is that a Big Mac is a Big Mac wherever you buy it, and you can buy Big Macs in 120 countries around the world. It should cost the same everywhere you go, but it doesn't. In the United States, the average cost of the burger is $3.00. However, in

China, you can buy one for only $1.26. That implies that the yuan is 58 percent undervalued compared to the U.S. dollar.

And that brings us to the theory of purchasing-power parity, which holds that, over the long run, exchange rates should move towards rates that would equalize the prices of an identical basket of goods and services in any two countries.

The International Monetary Fund agrees with the premise and claims that, by looking at the world through the lens of purchasing-power parity, we can explain the jump in commodity prices that we have seen. By the new yardstick, China accounts for one-third of global real GDP compared to only 13 percent contributed by the United States.

By focusing only on sluggish growth in America, we have been missing the big global picture. This new perception leads us to believe that emerging economies are not only growing much faster than rich economies and are more intensive in their use of raw materials and energy, but they also account for a bigger chunk of global output if measured correctly (reinforcing many of the points I have made throughout this book). To learn more about "burgernomics" and the Big Mac Index, visit the site of the *Economist* at www.economist.com.

Four Ways to Buy Dollar Insurance

If you have limited trading experience, an easy way to protect against a decline in the value of your dollars is to buy a CD denominated in a foreign currency. One way to do that is to open a World Currency account at Everbank (www.everbank.com), which will allow you to buy CDs denominated in twenty-five different currencies. These CDs are available in a variety of terms, from three month to one year, with a minimum investment of $10,000. Additionally, the CDs are FDIC insured. A CD denominated in another currency will not only diversify your portfolio, it will allow you to make capital gains if the U.S. dollar depreciates. Finally, many world currencies offer higher yields than what is available in CDs denominated in U.S. dollars. For example, at the time of this writing, New Zealand offered substantially higher yields than the United

States. By investing in a CD denominated in the New Zealand dollar, you would make 70 percent more interest, plus the potential for capital gains.

If you prefer greater diversification, Everbank offers index CDs in three-month and six-month terms that require a minimum investment of $20,000. One, the Prudent Central Bank CD, is designed to seek higher yields and potential capital gains from currencies backed by strong, inflation-fighting central banks. Another, the Petrol CD, is denominated in the currencies of Norway, England, and Mexico — all of which should benefit from strength in the oil sector. A third index CD, the Commodity CD, consists of the currencies of New Zealand, Canada, Australia, and South Africa – all countries whose currencies should benefit from rising commodity prices. Here is a summary of basic dollar hedging strategies.

- Buy a CD denominated in a foreign currency.
- Buy a Prudent Central Bank CD.
- Buy a Petrol CD.
- Buy a Commodity CD.

Why Borrowing Money Can Make Sense

When you buy a CD, a T-bill, a bond, or any other financial instrument where you give someone else money in return for interest, you have purchased a debt instrument. The party who took your money has promised to pay you back your money plus interest for the use of it. When you enter into this type of transaction, you have taken on the risk that, by the time the borrower returns your money, it will purchase less than it would today. Money, after all, is nothing more than purchasing power. In fact, if you begin to think of your money that way, it may be helpful to you. In most cases, if someone returns money to you at some time in the future, it will have less purchasing power than it does today.

As the coming inflation becomes more pronounced, you can be even more assured that the money you give away, in return for a paltry amount of interest, will most certainly have lost some of its purchasing power by the time you get it back. That is why — especially while interest rates have been low — I have chosen to borrow as much money as possible rather than lend it out. Here is why.

After the stock market crashed in 2000, the Federal Reserve opened the spigots, flooding the economy with money to prevent a recession, which would have surely occurred if they had not. In fact, the money supply increase began in earnest as early as 1995. In the last ten years, the broad money supply (M3) has doubled. The Fed channeled a large portion of that money (credit) through Fannie Mae and Freddie Mac, whose business it is to guarantee loans issued by banks and mortgage companies. The implicit government guarantees bestowed upon these two institutions by the federal government allowed banks and mortgage companies to lend money without recourse.

This, of course, suited the Federal Reserve, who understood that only consumer spending, which now accounts for almost ninety percent of GDP, could keep the economy afloat. However, consumers were already deeply in debt. Additionally, with over one and one-half million jobs lost to China and India since 1989, and with little hope of substantial wage increases for those still working, the consumer certainly did not have the ability to stimulate the economy. He needed assistance.

The Federal Reserve also knew that the housing market was critical to the survival of the economy. If the housing market stumbled, the entire economy would implode. The solution, then, was to nourish the housing market with cheap mortgage money. This would benefit the economy through a chain of events. First-time homebuyers, who could qualify more easily, would start the ball rolling. Move-up buyers could then sell their homes and afford to buy more expensive ones. Other homebuyers would simply take advantage of low-interest equity credit lines to remodel their current homes and pay off credit card debt, free-ing up even more spending power.

It was not hard to figure out that real estate prices would benefit. Housing and land in many parts of the country are in short supply. More money chasing too few homes is bound to bid up the prices. Moreover, many investors realized that fact also. The combination of investors and non-investors all bidding for the same limited supply of housing natu-rally caused prices to rise. For example, in one year, I bought a dozen houses — something I would not have done if it had not been so easy to borrow money. As a result of my purchases, twelve other families were crowded out of the market, eventually having to pay a higher price for home ownership. We will explore the topic of real estate in much more detail in chapter 11. However, before getting too far afield, let us get back to why it is not a good idea to lend your money to someone else in this environment.

Why Lending Money Is a Gamble

When you lend money, the longer you have to wait for the return of that money, the more risk you take that your money will be worth less when the borrower returns it to you. The bond market, until now, has held up primarily because of the largesse of the Japanese and Chinese, who have willingly lent us money by purchasing our federal debt. As we learned, they do this in order to keep their currencies from rising against the dollar and ruining their export trade business, which would plunge their economies into recession. However, foreign inflows of capital will decline once the rest of the world realizes that because we are hopelessly in debt, our economy risks a sharp decline without continued stimulus.

I know that is hard for you to accept. Americans are a prideful and nationalistic people. We built the greatest country in the world in two centuries and our history is something for which all Americans can be proud. However, by studying the economic history of our country, you will realize that we have had many booms and busts. People have made fortunes and people have lost fortunes. It is not a sign of lack of patriotism to protect yourself and your family from economic downturns or, in this case, inflation.

In the coming economic cycle, some individuals will thrive, as investors did who correctly positioned themselves in real estate and commodities in the early 1970s, and then moved their assets to stocks and bonds in the early 1980s. Those who fail to act will witness the value of their investments shrink and their lifestyles decline. Young people risk losing their jobs to overseas workers, trained to do the same job for a fraction of the wage an American would require. Boomers risk a decline in purchasing power of their retirement accounts and their other invest-

Table 8.1 Major Risks You Face

Young person	You risk losing your job to outsourcing and offshoring and you risk not being able to afford the rising costs of assets and services
Boomer	You risk losing your job to outsourcing and offshoring and you risk a decline in purchasing power of your accumulated savings and investments
Retiree	You risk losing purchasing power from your fixed income and savings, plus you face skyrocketing medical costs

ments, while the elderly will find that their fixed incomes simply will not afford them a decent lifestyle.

The United States has misappropriated its resources, squandered its wealth, and left its coming generation saddled with unmanageable debt. You can choose to put on blinders and hold fast to ideas of what America used to be, or you can educate yourself to the global realities of population trends, industrialization trends, and the massive shifts in wealth that are occurring. The world's capital will be drawn to the East like moths to a flame. The attraction will be cheaper labor and resources, an increasingly educated and skilled work force, and rising income and consumption patterns.

Countries grow stronger and richer by leaving more capital stock — means of production — to the next generation. Because we inherit means of production, such as buildings and factories, each generation begins with a higher standard of living than the next. Once that trend reverses, we are in trouble. Here is a hypothetical example of how capital stock evaporates.

Pretend that your father inherited a small widget factory from your grandfather. From only three employees, he grew the factory to thirty-five employees. Your father died and left the factory to his three children, you being the middle child. Your older brother was left to run the factory. However, due to competition from overseas, where widgets can be produced more cheaply, the factory is losing money. The three of you decide to close the factory and sell to a developer who will build condominiums on the site.

After deciding to escrow a portion of the proceeds to cover your mother's nursing home bills, you divide the remainder among the three of you. Your brother buys a sailboat, your sister remodels her home, and you use your share to pay college tuitions for your two children. The money is gone, the capital stock is gone, and your kids have to start from scratch. That is what is occurring everyday in this country and our government cannot stop the trend. Those in power can artificially support the economy only by pumping more money into the system. That means that the money you have now will be worth less in the future. Why would you want to give it to someone else who will give it back to you later when it is worth less?

Six Ways to Buy Insurance against Rising Interest Rates

I hope you are convinced that lending money — that is, purchasing notes and bonds — puts you at risk. If you have lent money, there are many ways to hedge that risk. Alternatively, if you are not at risk, you can use the following strategies to make speculative bets against rising interest rates.

You can use ETFs to protect yourself against rising interest rates. Your first option is to short either the IEF or the TLT. The IEF is an ETF that holds bonds maturing in seven to ten years and the TLT is an ETF that holds bonds maturing in twenty to thirty years. If you own bonds in your portfolio, this position would act to hedge your exposure. Remember, the bonds you are holding will decline in value as interest rates move up to keep pace with inflation. If you do not own bonds, shorting either of these ETFs would be a speculative play that would allow you to profit from declining bond prices. You can also hedge your interest-rate exposure by buying certain funds offered by Rydex and Profunds. Buying the Juno fund at Rydex is analogous to shorting the thirty-year bond. At Profunds, you can buy the Rising Rates fund.

You now have four easy ways to "buy insurance" against rising interest rates. Buy the TLT, the IEF, the Juno fund, and the Rising Rates fund. By hedging your bond portfolio, you can still collect interest without worrying that the price of your bonds will decline. Furthermore, if you

Table 8.2 Hedging Interest-Rate Risk

Short the IEF	Hedges money lent maturing in 7-10 years
Short the TLT	Hedges money lent maturing in 20-30 years
Buy the Juno fund	A mutual fund that gains when long-term rates rise
Buy the Rising Rates fund	A mutual fund that gains when long-term rates rise
Short T-bonds or T-notes in the futures market	Should only be used by experienced traders
Buy puts on T-bond and T-note futures	Should only be used by experienced traders

have a speculative nature, you may be able to use these vehicles to profit handsomely. Sophisticated traders can also hedge exposure to interest-rate risk by shorting T-bond and T-note futures contracts or buying puts on those contracts.

In this chapter, you learned how to save your purchasing power by hedging your dollar risk in financial assets that you may own, such as stocks and bonds. You also learned how to protect yourself against rising interest rates. In the next chapter, you are going to learn that select industries and certain companies will actually benefit from the crises that lie ahead and, more importantly, how you can cash in right alongside them.

9

How to Profit from the Dollar's Decline

The arrogance of officialdom should be tempered and controlled, and assistance to foreign hands should be curtailed, lest Rome fall.[1]

~ Marcus Tullius Cicero

Once upon a time, there was a great country, known throughout the world as a superpower. It dominated the world in nearly every area — finance, economics, and military strength. However, like Rome, this empire found itself overextended, with its military scattered in far-flung places across the globe. Once the most productive country in the world, over the years it produced less of the products that its citizens needed and imported more and more of its goods from more productive countries in faraway lands. With fewer factories to produce what the country needed, skilled laborers found themselves without work. The government could not raise enough in taxes to do all the things it wanted to do, like keep its troops stationed throughout the world, so it decided to borrow the money from those countries that had more. After a while, the superpower found itself with a large and growing federal deficit and a trade deficit as well.

One day the rest of the world began to worry about the policies of the superpower. They became worried that the superpower would never repay their loans or that they would try to get out of them by simply devaluing their currency through inflation. Eventually, when the other countries decided to take their capital home, rather than continue to finance this profligate nation, the superpower collapsed, never again to regain its former glory.

Did you guess the country in the story? It was Great Britain and the era was around 1910. Subsequently, the mantel passed to America, a country that produced more than it consumed. Great Britain had become a superpower the same way centuries earlier. China will be the next superpower for the same reason. Countries become great when they attract capital, produce goods, and export more than they import. Countries grow weak when they run deficits and import more than they export. When imports exceed exports, it is a sign that the country is not productive enough to provide for its population.

In America, we are rapidly losing our manufacturing base. Factories are closing and millions of jobs are being lost. The country is not increasing its capital stock. In fact, since the year 2000, the portion of investment capital that expands the capital stock has dropped by 60 percent. Americans need to save and invest more, instead of borrowing money to buy things that they do not really need. The country's economy is the sum of the individual actions of its populace. If Americans saved more, those savings — with sufficient incentives — could find their way to capital investment, which would allow America to rebuild its manufacturing base. A strong manufacturing base acts as a powerful economic stimulus because business spending has a ripple effect throughout the economy and puts people to work.

While well intended, government initiatives to promote savings and encourage capital spending have not born fruit, and the trends that I have outlined in this book remain firmly in place. Therefore, I expect more inflation. How will inflation affect the stock market? In general, inflation normally affects the stock market adversely. However, you need

Table 9.1 Globally Uncompetitive U.S. Industries

Toys, games, and sporting goods	We import six times as much as we export
ADP equipment and office machines	We buy three times as much from foreign competitors as from American producers
Televisions and VCRs	We import four times as much as we export

to remember that the stock market is a market of stocks. Even in bear markets, some individual companies prosper and make good investments. Going forward, how well a company can grow profits in an inflationary environment will determine its attractiveness.

Seven Stocks That Will Survive the Dollar's Decline

We hear a lot about the growing trade deficit and the fact that China can produce nearly anything more cheaply than we can make it in the United States. However, that is only partially true. If we look at broad trade categories, the picture appears bleak: overall, we import more consumer goods, industrial supplies, automotive vehicles, capital goods, and food than we export. Table 9.1 looks at a few industries within those broad trade categories where America is taking a beating from foreign competition.

However, while we are slipping behind in most industries, we still can do some things better than anyone else in the world. Complex and expensive machinery is one example and a primary reason why capital equipment is our leading export. Here are several industries where we manage to produce and export more than we import.

- airplanes
- chemicals
- coal
- corn
- cotton
- metal ores
- scientific instruments
- specialized industrial machinery.

It would make sense to invest only in American companies that can compete on a global scale. For example, almost no other country has the technology to compete with us in aerospace. I say almost because Europe is a very close second. We also excel in the chemical industry. In agriculture, we are holding our own in corn and cotton production. In mining, we have a strong position in coal and metal ores. Finally, we still have a slight global advantage in the production of scientific instruments and specialized machinery.

Now that we have identified areas where we are competitive, the next step is to think about whether those industries are likely to grow in the years ahead. Given the fact that most of the world is just entering a stage of rapid industrialization, nearly all of our selected industries should do well. Furthermore, if we expect the dollar to fall in value, those industries that have proven themselves as export oriented and globally competitive should gain even more market share as their products become more competitively priced on the world market. Now, let us try to find a few good companies that find themselves in that fortunate position.

- *Boeing (BA)*

  Boeing is a company worth investigating for several reasons. First, it is the world's largest defense contractor. Second, it is a huge multinational corporation with customers in 145 countries. Third, it is the global market leader in military aircraft, satellites, launch systems, and missile defense. Finally, it is the country's largest exporter. As the dollar declines, all of Boeing's military hardware and aircraft will become cheaper to foreign purchasers. Therefore, sales should rise.

  However, approximately 40 percent of Boeing's revenues are non-defense related and come from its commercial airline division. Boeing has nearly 13,000 commercial jetliners in service worldwide, which is roughly 75 percent of the world fleet. If the global airline industry grows, Boeing will benefit. However, Boeing's commercial airline division could stumble because of two unknowns. First, higher oil prices could cause commercial airline companies to falter or fail, thus affecting demand for Boeing's airplanes. Second, their European rival, Airbus, could gain market share. Weigh the positives against the potential negatives carefully before deciding to invest.

- *Peabody Energy (BTU)*
  Peabody Energy is the world's largest coal company and provides 10 percent of the electricity for the United States. It was recently named the coal company of the year at the Global Energy Awards ceremony. We discussed the company in some detail earlier when we looked for companies that would benefit from growing energy demand. Now, we consider Peabody in a different light – as a major exporter that should profit from a lower dollar.

- *Dupont (DD)*
  Dupont is a major, multinational chemical company, which has operations in seventy-five countries and derives more than half of its sales from outside the United States. Because of that, this leading exporter should also benefit from a weaker dollar. Its core business is specialty manufacturing, and it holds over 22,000 worldwide patents and 2,100 unique trademarks. The largest grossing segment of its business is agriculture and nutrition, a global growth area. Because of one of its wholly owned subsidiaries, Dupont is the world's largest seed producer. Like many other companies, however, Dupont's input costs could rise if energy costs move substantially higher.

- *U.S. Steel (X), Nucor (NUE), and AK Steel (AKS)*
  Steel is one of the industries that built this country and will be a prominent industry in global industrialization. Each of these three big companies is a heavyweight and tends to acquire smaller companies. While the demand for steel is growing voraciously in China, a domestic or global recession could hurt profits. Therefore, make certain that global economic winds are at your back before making long-term commitments in this sector.

- *Bunge Limited (BG)*
  Bunge Limited is a multinational food company whose principle activity is to sell agricultural and food products. It processes and sells grains and oil seeds and also manufactures and markets veg-

etable oil. Another segment of the company manufactures and markets products derived from wheat and corn. Finally, it mines raw materials for use in fertilizer production. Bunge will benefit from the growing global demand for food and should benefit from a lower dollar.

Table 9.2 summarizes the seven stocks that should survive the dollar's decline.

Forex Trading

An even more direct way to profit from the dollar's decline is to take all the trading in all the stock markets in the world and multiply that by 32.5. That is how big the foreign exchange market (FOREX) is. Welcome to the world's largest casino, the only market in the world where you can trade without paying commission. Unlike the stock market or futures markets, the brokerage firm or bank that you deal through makes their money via the spread, just as a specialist would on the New York Stock Exchange. Spreads in FOREX, quoted in pips, run 3 to 5 pips, which equates to about .03 percent of the total dollar value of the trade. In comparison, spreads on both stock trades and futures trades run .04 − .06 percent of the total. Finally, because the margin requirement is only 1 percent, you get more bang for your buck.

What can you trade in the FOREX market? Some of the most common foreign currencies are the Eurodollar, Japanese yen, British pound, Swiss franc, Canadian dollar, Australian dollar, and New Zealand dollar, but there are many others. Foreign currencies are traded in pairs. When you buy Japanese yen, for example, you simultaneously sell U.S. dollars. Therefore, you have entered a spread trade: long the yen and short the dollar. You can trade other pairs outside the dollar as well. For example, you could put on a trade long yen and short British pounds.

If inflation goes higher in the United States, the value of the dollar will drop against other currencies. Therefore, in the FOREX market you might want to consider the following positions.

- short dollar/long yen

Table 9.2 Multinationals Positioned to Benefit from a Weaker Dollar

Boeing	BA	World's largest defense contractor
Peabody Energy	BTU	World's largest coal company
Dupont	DD	Big in agriculture and nutrition
U.S. Steel	X	Major steel company
Nucor	NUE	Major steel company
AK Steel	AKS	Major steel company
Bunge	BG	Major agricultural producer

- short dollar/long Swiss franc
- short dollar/long Australian dollar
- short dollar/long New Zealand dollar
- short dollar/long Canadian dollar

For those who do have technical trading skills, FOREX is very accessible even to the small trader with as little as $5,000 to invest. There is no formal exchange, but simply by typing FOREX into your search engine you will find a wealth of information. If you do not have those skills, however, you may want to develop them over time before venturing into FOREX trading. That does not mean that you cannot benefit from the inevitable decline in the dollar. Simply stick with the investment vehicles you learned about in chapter 5.

Here are the primary advantages of FOREX trading.

1. Profit from the dollar's decline.
2. Maximum leverage.
3. Commission-free trading.
4. Excellent liquidity (narrow bid/ask spreads).

10

How to Profit from the Global Arms Race

The first panacea for a mismanaged nation is inflation of the currency; the second is war. Both bring a temporary prosperity; both bring a permanent ruin. Both are the refuge of political and economic opportunists.[1]

~ Ernest Hemingway

While ideological differences may contribute to armed conflicts in the future, military conflicts will increasingly find their genesis in fights for possession or control of vital resources needed for the functioning of modern societies. Countries understand that to survive and prosper, they will need to have strong economies, and that, without the inputs to production, those goals will not be attainable. Many nations have already stated their intentions regarding their defense of vital interests.

The first warning came from the United States in 1980. The Carter doctrine stated:

"An attempt by an outside force to gain control of the Persian Gulf region will be regarded as an assault on the vital interests of America, and will be repelled by any means necessary, including military force."

More recently, Russia issued a similar warning in a military doctrine approved by President Putin. "The functions of Russia's armed forces include creation of the conditions for the security of economic activity and protection of the Russian Federation's national interests in the territorial seas, on the continental shelf, and in the exclusive offshore economic zone of the Russian Federation and on the high seas."[3]

Both China and Japan have made their intentions known regarding the vital South China Sea region. In 1995, China's Prime Minister, Li Peng, declared that the People's Liberation Army must strengthen its air and naval capabilities to "safeguard the sovereignty and territorial integrity of the motherland and our maritime rights and interests."[4] Meanwhile, in 1996, Tokyo adopted a new national defense program outline that calls on Japanese forces to enhance their capacity to protect essential sea-lanes and other critical interests in the waters surrounding Japan.[5]

In the future, the competition for limited natural resources will intensify. There is an ever-growing demand for a wide range of basic commodities and certain key materials that all industrial societies require. As we have learned, many important resources are not renewable, and limited supplies exist. Each year, the planet adds another 80 million people. As the population grows, the world consumes more. As the economies of China and India industrialize, their demands for infrastructure, factories, and transportation place an even greater burden on the remaining supplies of certain critical natural resources.

Ensuring U.S access to overseas supplies of vital resources has become a central theme of American security policy and military planning. Military operations, base-building and forward deployment has taken place almost exclusively in geographic areas of vital resources — the most obvious being the Persian Gulf and Caspian Sea region. Moreover, the defense of oil fields and maritime trade routes is now the central focus of military planning.

All the major countries of the world realize that they need a steady, reliable flow of essential resources in order for their economies to prosper. Only military power can ensure the security and uninterrupted flow of those resources. Therefore, expect a worldwide buildup of the military in all countries that are able to afford to buy arms. This buildup has already begun.

The United States now has troops based in one hundred countries, with over 250,000 troops stationed in the critical Gulf region. If the Middle East had no oil, do you honestly believe that we would spend hundreds of billions of dollars to ensure the freedom of Iraqis? I can assure you that anywhere there is energy and vital natural resources, the United States will find a reason to send troops there. I can also assure you that you will see higher military budgets in this country every single year well into the future. In fact, I will put my money on that bet.

"Rebuilding America's Defenses" (RAD) provides a clear blueprint for the future course of military spending. Consider this quote from the document: "Preserving the desirable strategic situation in which the United States now finds itself requires a globally preeminent military capability both today and in the future."[6]

You can read the document on the Project for the New American Century's website (www.newamericancentury.org). The document calls for increased military spending and a dramatic transformation of both military technology and the role of the military. The neoconservatives, now in power, advocate massive spending to upgrade our military technology and expand the number of military bases — both deployment and forward operating bases — throughout the world.

The RAD document was written in the year 2000. Since then, the military budget has increased by 30 percent and forward bases have begun springing up everywhere — in nine countries neighboring Afghanistan, as well as in Bulgaria, Uzbekistan, Turkey, Kuwait, and more. Sixty thousand military personnel now call these bases home.

While oil is the commodity of most strategic interest to the United States, for other countries, water is their greatest concern. Many countries in the Middle East and North Africa lack sufficient supplies of water to meet the needs of their growing populations. Countries will clash over the fresh waters of the Nile, the Jordan River, the Tigris, and the Euphrates. The population in the Nile River basin is increasing by millions of people each year. To prevent famines, the region needs more agriculture and irrigated fields.

Disputes are bound to arise as to who actually owns the water of the Nile and other major rivers. For example, the Nile carries water through nine countries, and the Euphrates through three. The countries controlling the upstream portions of these (and many other) rivers can use their military power to allocate more water to their own people at the expense of downstream countries.

Future conflicts and military engagements over fresh water are a near certainty, but countries will fight over other natural resources as well. Disputes are already occurring over diamonds, minerals, and timber in many parts of the world. Without going into the details of specific conflicts, we can safely assume that the governments involved will attempt to arm themselves to the teeth as the conflicts over natural resources intensify.

Another problem lies in determining who owns what. For example, six different countries claim dominion over parts of the South China Sea. Vast quantities of oil and natural gas could lie below this large expanse of water. Each country has an exclusive economic zone (EEZ) extending out 200 miles from their borders. However, when countries claim to own islands out in the middle, determining the EEZ boundaries becomes quite difficult. The most hotly contested area is the Spratly Islands — some four hundred tiny islands distributed over 80,000 square miles of ocean. These islands are claimed in whole or in part by Brunei, China, Malaysia, the Philippines, Taiwan, and Vietnam.

To defend this area, as well as shipping lanes, China is developing a growing flotilla of large oceangoing warships equipped with modern Russian and Western missile systems. It has purchased destroyers, surface-to-air missiles, amphibious assault vessels, and combat planes. In a joint venture with Russia, it hopes to build a modern aircraft carrier.

All of Southeast Asia is now in a naval arms race. Malaysia, whose goal is to have the largest navy in the region, has purchased missile corvettes from Italy and frigates from Scotland. Its domestic shipbuilding now puts it in the lead of all naval construction in Southeast Asia. Not to be outdone, Thailand has recently acquired its first aircraft carrier. The Thais have also purchased frigates from the United States and patrol boats from Australia. Meanwhile, Indonesia is planning to buy the entire navy of the former East Germany. While I will leave out the specifics, both Singapore and Brunei are expanding their navies at a similar breakneck pace. Moreover, all of these countries have acquired long-range patrol planes and fighter aircraft to complement their navies.

With all this going on around them, Japan — a country almost totally dependent on outside sources for energy — has reason to worry. In response to the naval buildups of other Asian countries, the Japanese have invested heavily in maritime defense by developing new warships, destroyers, frigates, and assault ships. However, at this time, Japan's best defense of the region lies with the U.S. Seventh Fleet, based in Yokosuka, Japan.

While we can expect the Middle East to remain a powder keg for decades to come, the South China Sea is also a likely area for military confrontations. Because of the many countries vying for control of the region and their political alliances, it would not take much of a spark to ignite a serious conflagration. In addition, the Caspian Sea region — with its huge potential oil and natural gas deposits — is another powder keg. Finally, Africa, while poor and politically corrupt, is home to much of the world's natural resource wealth. Eventually, larger, more powerful countries will compete for it.

While the United States remains decades ahead of any other country in the arms race, the fact is that wealth is flowing from west to east. With wealth, comes power. Who could have imagined that Indonesia would one day buy the entire East German navy? As the Asian countries become wealthier, they will have the ability to buy the technology and armaments that they need to aggressively compete with the world's industrialized nations. One thing is certain. Paralleling the scramble for vital resources is the trend toward global armament. Defense spending is on the rise. Is there a way that we can profit from that knowledge?

Four Battle-Tested Stocks

When it comes to building fighting machines, the United States is still at the forefront of the technology. Just as Exxon Mobile and Chevron-Texaco dominate the world's corporate landscape for energy production, the United States is home to several of the world's largest defense contractors. We will not need to go too far from home to find companies that will benefit from the new global arms race. I will detail several companies whose business it is to produce the weapons of modern military conflict, and that should profit from increased defense spending.

1. *Northrop Grumman (NOC)*
   Northrop Grumman, headquartered in Los Angeles, is involved in almost every aspect of defense. It is the largest shipbuilder for the U.S. military and the second largest defense contractor. Having acquired TRW in 2002, it is well positioned in the field of defense electronics — an area expected to be very much in demand in the future. Its Newport News sector is one of only two companies capable of designing and building nuclear-powered submarines. Finally, its space technology sector is a leader in space-based defense systems.

2. *General Dynamics (GD)*
   General Dynamics has four main business segments: aerospace, combat systems, information systems, and marine systems. It produces many products that countries could use for national defense, such as ships, land and amphibious combat machines, armored vehicles, gun systems, and submarines. If I am half-right about the future, those products could be in great demand. General Dynamics also supplies construction materials to the Middle East. It seems that this company makes money, not only from supplying the tools of war, but also from the destruction.

3. *Lockheed Martin (LMT)*
   Lockheed Martin, the country's largest defense contractor, does 80

percent of its business with the U.S. government. The number and kinds of products it makes is too long to list. However, it is fair to say that Lockheed Martin is the leader in many products used in the defense industry. Furthermore, because of its size and profitability, it is capable of making acquisitions whenever smaller companies become available. Unless peace breaks out all over, Lockheed Martin's prospects seem bright.

4. *United Defense Industries (UDI)*

United Defense Industries is a pure play on U.S. combat. United Defense Industries has been making landing craft and armored vehicles since World War II. They are a leader in the design, development, and production of combat vehicles, artillery, naval guns, missile launchers, and precision munitions. They are famous for their Bradley armored infantry vehicle, and they make self-propelled howitzers and amphibious assault vehicles. The U.S. government is their primary customer, making up 80 percent of their sales.

A second reason to believe that an investment in United Defense makes sense is because of the company's investors. The Carlyle Group owns 49.5 percent of United Defense Industries. This investment group, with more than $12 billion in assets, operates within the so-called iron triangle of industry, government, and the military. The top people in the company include former President Bush, the former Secretary of Defense, the former Secretary of State, and the former Prime Minister of England. According to Dan Briody, author of *The Iron Triangle: Inside the Secret World of the Carlyle Group*, "Carlyle has established itself as the gatekeeper between private business interests and U.S. defense spending."[7]

80 Million More Mouths to Feed

While the stocks of most companies go down during commodity bull markets, companies connected to the commodity business can do quite well. The 80 million people who join the global community each year will require food, which will require more agriculture. As commodity prices

Table 10.1 Companies Positioned to Profit from Military Conflict

Northrop Grumman	NOC	Involved in every aspect of defense
General Dynamics	GD	Produces the tools for war and the construction materials for rebuilding
Lockheed Martin	LMT	America's largest defense contractor
United Defense Industries	UDI	Pure play on U.S. combat

rise, farmers will become more profitable. With their profits, they will buy machinery to increase efficiency in an attempt to meet the world's growing demand for food. Manufacturers of heavy machinery used in agriculture should benefit.

Two companies positioned to profit are Caterpillar (CAT) and John Deere (DE). Caterpillar, a Fortune 100 company, is the world's leading manufacturer of construction and mining equipment, diesel and natural gas engines, and industrial gas turbines. Meanwhile, John Deere, in business since 1837, is now a worldwide operation doing business in 160 countries. John Deere has been the world's premier producer of agricultural equipment since 1963. It is also the world's leading manufacturer of forestry equipment and a major manufacturer of construction equipment such as loaders, graders, and excavators.

Final Thoughts on Multinationals, Defense, and Agriculture

Increasingly, the United States is heading down the same path traveled by Great Britain early in the twentieth century. We have allowed our manufacturing base to decline, while growing more indebted and dependent on foreign countries. While some of the proposed solutions are encouraging, the realty of the situation is that the patchwork of ideas put forth will not be sufficient to overcome the perfect financial storm that is heading our way.

The United States is still the world leader in many industries and prominent companies in those industries will likely benefit from the third world's industrialization process and the attendant rise in demand

Table 10.2 Companies Positioned to Profit from Commodity Bull Markets

Caterpillar	CAT	World leader in construction and mining equipment
John Deere	DE	World leader in agricultural equipment

for specialized industrial products. Additionally, the growing world population will provide demand for food producers and manufacturers. Investments in those types of companies make sense given expectations of rising inflation and a declining dollar.

While not highly publicized, a global armaments race is underway. The impetus is the perceived need by countries to secure supplies and distribution routes of natural resources. As supplies become scarcer, conflicts will intensify. Defense budgets are rising, not only in the United States, but throughout the world. America is the world leader in military equipment, and several companies in the defense sector will probably do quite well in the future.

The worldwide growth in agriculture is a given. Companies that specialize in growing food or in technologies that optimize crop yields have a good chance of profiting. As the world's agricultural business grows to meet the demands of a growing world population, companies such as Caterpillar and John Deere that make the tools used in agriculture should benefit.

In the next chapter, we will turn our attention to real estate. If you are like most Americans, the majority of your net worth is in real estate. Is it safe? Because real estate, unlike stocks, is a localized investment, I cannot provide you with that answer. However, I will help you find the answer by detailing the factors that will contribute to future price determination and presenting arguments by both real estate bulls and real estate bears. One thing is certain; real estate is no different from any other market in one respect: prices can go up, down, or sideways. You need to learn how to protect yourself in case prices decline. Happily, you are just minutes away from learning how to do that. In addition, you are about to learn how to make big profits from a decline in real estate prices by using the little-known investments presented in the next chapter.

How to Protect Your Real Estate

It's tangible, it's solid, it's beautiful. It's artistic, from my standpoint, and I just love real estate.[1]

~ Donald Trump

When you read this book, real estate prices could be rising, falling, or flat. Moreover, prices could be rising in some areas of the country and falling in other areas. It will not matter. Real estate will continue to be your best hedge against inflation over the long run. However, real estate goes through cycles. This chapter will show you how to hedge your real estate investments so that you will be protected during downturns.

Everyone Has a Real Estate Story

Growing up, I remember my parents talking about real estate they could have bought at some time when they were younger. Unfortunately, they did not. When the subject of real estate came up during a backyard barbeque with neighbors, my parents would wax nostalgic about the time they could have bought such and such for only so many dollars. It seemed the more distant the memory, the more incredible would have been the eventual gain. My favorite story was the one about the ocean-front lot — now worth several million dollars — that they had a chance to buy for $5,000 in 1956. Equally incredulous was the story about the ten acres of prime lakefront (now going for $10,000 a front foot) that my grandfather had a chance to buy in the 1920s for $2,000.

When I was a child, the stories gave me hope. Wow, we almost could have been rich! It was as though life were a game of horseshoes, and proximity counted. By the time I was old enough to realize that proximity really did not count, the stories took on the emotional overtones of a cruel joke. In fact, I wanted to strangle my parents — figuratively speaking, of course — whenever they told them. Of course, when talk turns to real estate, everyone has a story. My parents' friends had similar tales, so it was not as though my parents were the lone idiots on the block.

How to Put Your Money on Ice

Chances are quite good that your house is the single biggest and best investment you will ever make. Certainly, that is true for most people, but the question we need to ask ourselves is why. The answer is quite simple, although not readily apparent. To see it, you need to turn the telescope around and look backwards through it. By doing so, you can see that the price increases of your house have been, to a degree, an optical illusion.

What appeared to be the house rising in value over the years was nothing more than dollars depreciating over the same period. Housing was simply a convenient yardstick, which measured how much your other money shrunk over time. Viewed that way, you not only solve the mystery of rising home prices, but also can appreciate the cleverness of using housing as a hedge against inflation and a way to preserve purchasing power.

Why is housing unique in that respect? For one thing, silly as it may sound, China cannot manufacture your house and lot. Most likely, you live in a neighborhood with friendly neighbors, good schools, a library, a hospital, a fire department, and a police department. A grocery store, pharmacy, and a hospital are close by. Your house is more than a just a house. It is part of a unique community – one that cannot be replicated, and that is what gives value to your house.

Developers can build new houses, of course. However, a new house will cost more to build than your house did, and that will always be true — because the steel, lumber, copper, and cement that goes into building a new house will always cost more. Because the dollar depreciates steadily over time, labor costs rise also. Finally, environmental impact fees, which the developer passes on to the homebuyer, rise as well. Moreover, in any town, the first people there bought the most desirable lots, leaving Johnny-come-latelies to pay higher prices for less desirable locations. That is particularly true for waterfront.

By purchasing your house when you did, you froze the cost of all those inputs that go into building a house. You may not have thought of it that way, but it was no less miraculous than if you had taken a magic wand, waved it in front of your house, and stopped money from shrinking. If you paid $200,000 for your house, you were able to freeze the purchasing power of $200,000. The concept is nothing short of amazing.

Real Estate Bulls

Real estate bulls believe that housing prices will continue to rise for several good reasons. First, they always have. It is hard to dispute an unbroken chain of national average price increases every year going back as far as we have reliable data. That is a fundamental trend based on limited supply, the increasing costs of development, the increasing population, and continuous inflation. Bulls have good reasons to be bullish on real estate as an investment.

Additionally, real estate bulls take comfort in the fact that the Federal Reserve controls short-term interest rates, which are the basis for the rates on adjustable rate mortgages. Interest rates on fifteen-year and thirty-year fixed rate mortgages are based on the interest rate of the ten-year note, which responds to expectations of future inflation. If inflation expectations pick up, the rate on the ten-year note will rise, as will rates on fifteen-year and thirty-year mortgages. The bulls claim that, if rates on fixed rate mortgages rise too much relative to rates on adjustable mortgages, borrowers will simply opt for adjustable rate mortgages. Therefore, rising rates on longer term fixed rate mortgages would not be enough to kill the real estate market. The Federal Reserve set out the punch bowl of easy money, and only they can take it away.

Real estate bulls believe that the Federal Reserve cannot afford to crush the real estate market because doing so would have a devastating effect on the economy. The numbers certainly support that claim. For example, 70 percent of local tax revenue comes from real estate taxes. If property values decline, local municipalities and counties would face budget shortfalls, which would force them to cut back on services that we take for granted. Furthermore, if short-term interest rates rise, builders will find it harder to sell homes, and will cut back on building. Much of the economy is dependent on new homes as well as the appliances and furnishings that go into them. According to www.realtor.org, every one thousand new homes built generate 2,448 new jobs and $79.4 million dollars of wages.[2] In sum, housing accounts for a significant portion of GDP, and its ripple effect throughout the economy acts as a necessary stimulus. Pull the plug on housing and you guarantee a steep recession if not a depression. It's that simple.

Real Estate Bears

Real estate bears say that the real estate boom is really a bubble, pumped up by unsustainable credit creation. According to www.economy.com, a one-percentage movement in mortgage rates eliminates two and one-half million people from the home-buying market. Real estate bears believe that if first time homebuyers can no longer qualify to buy homes — either because of rising interest rates, rising home prices, or a combination of both — move-up buyers will not be able to sell their homes and move up. If that happened, the entire housing boom could come to a screeching halt.

Furthermore, when interest rates rise, every buyer is affected. For example, if mortgage interest rates rise from 6 percent to 8 percent, a buyer would now only qualify for a lower-priced home. It does not matter that his income has not changed. Taking the argument to its conclusion, home prices would have to adjust downward to match the new affordability requirements.

Bears believe that real estate's undoing will begin with marginal first-time buyers – those for whom housing costs require a significant portion of their income. According to the National Association of Realtors, 40 percent of all homes sold last year sold to first-time homebuyers. Recently, the Bush administration proudly pointed to their record of achieving the highest home ownership rates in history. While the fact is laudable, it could also represent the Achilles' heel of the entire housing boom.

One piece of evidence comes from the Mortgage Bankers Association of America (www.mortgagebankers.org), which shows that the mortgage foreclosure rate has been growing despite the fact that home prices are rising. Not surprisingly, foreclosure rates are the highest among sub-prime loans – the fastest growing segment of the mortgage origination business. If foreclosures are increasing in a strong real estate market during a period of low interest rates, bears warn that foreclosures could sky-rocket when interest rates rise and consumers find that their mortgage payments are suddenly 30 to 50 percent higher.

As many as nine million Americans have recently bought homes that they would not have been able to afford with traditional underwriting standards. These sub-prime borrowers pay higher interest rates and are seven times as likely to default on their mortgages. Furthermore, if home prices dip, those people could find themselves owing more on their homes than they are worth. With no equity in their homes, some will elect to walk away from high monthly payments and rent instead.

Elizabeth Warren, a Harvard law professor and one of the most respected bankruptcy-law experts in the country, claims that two-parent, middle-class, working families are on the brink of financial disaster. The reason, according to Warren, is that the wealthy baby boom generation has bid up the price of housing and related services to unmanageable levels. She argues that families have used easily available consumer credit and home equity loans to keep pace, but many families considered middle class are, in fact, insolvent.[3] In effect, the data shows that many Americans spend more than they make. To make up the difference, they borrow more — either on credit cards or by using the equity in their house. However, the result is that both their debt and monthly interest payments increase.

Finally, the economists at www.economy.com believe that the forces keeping the housing market rising are waning. In particular, they site the fact that the record number of sales during the past few years indicates that the demand for housing in nearly spent. In other words, those people who wanted a new or bigger house (suddenly affordable because of lower interest rates) have already bought.

Bullish and Bearish Real Estate Arguments

Bullish Arguments
1. Housing stock is low and developable land is limited.
2. The costs to develop land and build houses will continue to increase.
3. The population of the country is increasing.
4. The Federal Reserve is able to control short-term interest rates, which are the basis for the rates charged on adjustable rate mortgages.
5. The Federal Reserve has no choice but to support the housing market or face a severe recession.

Bearish Arguments
1. Higher interest rates or higher housing prices may soon price first-time buyers out of the market.
2. Recent first-time, sub-prime homebuyers face a growing risk of default.
3. Homeowners are highly in debt and at risk for default because of turning equity into debt through home equity loans.
4. The demand for more expensive homes by the move-up buyer is spent.

Real Estate's Sweet Spot

Regardless of what happens to mortgage rates, supply and demand will still determine the prices of houses. To understand supply and demand from a macro-economic perspective, you have to begin with demographics. The population of the United States is growing and existing housing stock is limited. A large portion of America's houses were constructed in the 1950s and 1960s and do not offer the conveniences of newer homes. Almost all Americans would live in bigger homes with more modern conveniences if they could afford to. Therefore, not withstanding cyclical downturns, we can expect the demand for new houses to remain strong for years to come.

Specific migration patterns in the United States, which are occurring now, will likely continue. In general, people are moving out of the Northeast and Midwest and moving to the West and the South. When you examine percentage gains in population, southern states win out. In fact, continued growth in Arizona, New Mexico, and Florida is a near certainty. While these may not be the only places that you can make money, risk is lowest and the potential for price appreciation is greatest in these areas.

Baby boomers are seeking either primary or second homes in a warm climate. These people want to fish, play golf, and go to the beach – not shovel snow and see the sun go down in the late afternoon. According to a recent census, more people are moving to Florida than any other state. The lure of Florida is so strong that even Californians are moving there. In fact, during the 1990s, 100,000 people moved from California to Florida, citing California's high cost of living, economic slump, high taxes, and pollution.[4]

A certain percentage of people will move to Florida as soon as they retire and the leading edge of the baby boom generation will be reaching retirement age in just a few years. Each year, as prices rise, more pre-retirees purchase their home in the sun while prices are still affordable. The question we need to answer is this: will retirees be able to afford to live in Florida?

To answer that question, let us profile a typical purchaser from the

Northeast, the area of origination for 90 percent of Floridians. Born in 1945, this hypothetical boomer bought a house in New England in 1980 when he was thirty-five years old. He paid $150,000 for the house. He is now sixty and the kids have graduated college and moved away. His home, almost paid for, is now worth $831,000. Additionally, he has accumulated $200,000 in savings. In a few years, he can expect an income from his pension and Social Security. He is a prime prospect for a retirement home in Florida. This data shows that affordability is not going to be an issue for the majority of boomers if they want to move to Florida. Let me reiterate my earlier proposition: regardless of what happens to mortgage interest rates, supply and demand will still determine the prices of houses. Retirees do not get mortgages; they pay cash.

An array of statistics supports the idea that prices will continue to rise along the east coast of Florida from West Palm Beach to Jacksonville. First, an ideal climate will attract population from other areas of the country. Second, retiring baby boomers will soon swell the ranks of those heading to Florida to buy either permanent or second homes. Third, the supply of land for development close to the ocean is limited and grows costlier every year. Finally, housing from West Palm Beach to Jacksonville is underpriced relative to many other parts of the country, especially populous states like New York, New Jersey, Connecticut, and California. Price increases are also likely to continue along Florida's west coast and, to a lesser extent, in Florida's interior as well.

Here are five reasons coastal Florida real estate makes sense.

1. Demand is relatively immune to interest rates because retirees pay cash.
2. An ideal climate will continue to be a magnet.
3. The demand for second homes will fuel demand for as much as two decades.
4. The supply of land near the ocean, especially in South Florida, is limited.
5. Prices are still reasonable relative to populous states such as New York, New Jersey, Connecticut, Massachusetts, and California.

Higher interests would certainly slow the rapid appreciation that we have seen in some parts of the country, such as in California and parts of

New England. When that happens, Florida real estate will not be immune. However, I believe that Florida real estate will weather any downturn far better than the aforementioned areas for reasons I have already elaborated. Additionally, because a large percentage of Florida residents are retired, a general economic downturn and rising unemployment levels will have a minimal effect on home prices. In Florida, demographic trends may outweigh the expected price setbacks that would normally accompany an economic downturn.

Purchasing real estate — and Florida real estate in particular — should provide a hedge against inflation. However, learning how to follow micro and macro real estate trends is fundamental to your success. In the next section, you will learn some easy ways to do that. On a final note, the real estate market changes quickly. To stay abreast of current trends and potential sweet spots for investing, visit the book's website at www.HoneyWhoShrunkOurMoney.com.

How to Monitor the Real Estate Market

If you owned a stock, you would want to track not only its performance but the performance of the overall stock market as well. You would also want to know how your stock was performing relative to other stocks in its industry. You can do the same in the real estate market. If you own a property, or are thinking of buying one, you can monitor its price performance both on a micro and macro level.

Starting on a micro level, you would want to keep track of the price trends in neighborhoods where you might want to purchase. The distinction between your neighborhood and the entire country is analogous to that of one stock versus the entire stock market. The neighborhoods where you plan to invest have their own fundamentals — such as their economic base, level of income and employment, and general desirability — that differentiate them from other neighborhoods in the country.

Here is a simple method you can use that will only take a few minutes each week. On Sunday, read your local newspaper's real estate classifieds and circle all the homes advertised in the neighborhoods you are considering. In a notebook, record the lowest, highest, and average price of homes advertised for sale. You may find that performing this exercise once a month is adequate. If you are ambitious enough, you can even chart the prices on a graph. By doing this, you will learn a lot about real estate values in the neighborhoods you follow. You may also want to monitor rents in those neighborhoods so that you will know what rental income to expect if you intend to use the property as an investment.

Another way to get price information is to use www.realtor.com. One disadvantage is that the site only contains MLS (Multiple Listing Service) listings. A second disadvantage is that the geographical breakdown is sometimes not as detailed as in the local newspaper. However, realtors often do not advertise their properties in the local newspaper. Therefore, to get a complete picture, use both resources. One enterprising realtor I know e-mails a list of all properties listed and sold in my area during the past thirty days. This saves me from having to do the research on my own. Try to find a realtor in your area who does the same. Now that you know how to follow prices on a micro level, you need to know what is happening to the housing market on a macro level.

The National Association of Realtors publishes some good housing data on their website, www.realtor.org. The first data set of interest is the existing single-family home sales. In that table, you can track the number of homes sold each month in each section of the country. It also shows the number of homes available for sale and the number of months' supply of homes on the market, a very important statistic. If supply begins to rise significantly, it is an early warning that sellers will soon reduce their asking prices.

Two additional important tables you can find on the site are the sales price of existing single-family homes and the Housing Affordability Index. The first table tracks the average price of a home in the Northeast, Midwest, South, and West each month. To calculate the Housing Affordability Index, the government combines data from the average cost of housing (sale prices) with both current financing statistics and median family incomes to determine what percentage of an average family's income would be required to pay for an average house. The logic is that if houses are too expensive in an area relative to the income of the population, housing prices may adjust downwards. Conversely, in some

Table 11.1 How to Monitor the Real Estate Market

Existing single-family home sales	www.realtor.org	Watch how many months supply on market to anticipate future trends
Sales price of existing single-family homes	www.realtor.org	Track the average sales price by region
Housing Affordability Index	www.realtor.org	Track prices relative to income and current financing rates
Housing Price Index	www.ofheo.gov	See 245 MSAs ranked by price appreciation

areas, housing prices may have room to rise. As you might imagine, in the West, housing costs have outstripped the average family's ability to pay. However, in the Midwest, families could afford higher prices.

The Office of Federal Housing Enterprise Oversight's (www.ofheo.gov) Housing Price Index is a good source of information for national housing appreciation trends, as well as for trends in individual states and metropolitan areas. The OFHEO compiles this index quarterly. The Housing Price Index contains rankings of all states by price appreciation, the percentage change in appreciation over different periods, and a ranking of 245 metropolitan statistical areas (MSAs) by house appreciation.

Using the Housing Price Index, you can examine national quarterly and yearly appreciation numbers dating back to 1990. Interestingly, if you compare any quarter to the same quarter one year earlier, the percentage of appreciation is always positive, resulting in a data set of sixty consecutive positive numbers. You can also view house appreciation by state going back to 1980. By comparing states over different periods, you can get a good idea of trends in different areas of the country. As an added bonus, the OFHEO ranks the states by current annual appreciation percentages.

How to Hedge Your Real Estate Risk

Real estate is a regional business. There will always be people who have cash and desire to live in a particular place. Rising interest rates or the foreclosure rate of marginal buyers may have little effect on them. Buying well-located real estate at the right price will always make sense. Nevertheless, why take chances? There are ways to hedge your real estate exposure and potentially profit handsomely if the housing market should fall.

What would have to occur for the real estate bears to be right? Interest rates would have to rise appreciably. Therefore, the logical way to hedge against falling real estate prices is to short interest rate contracts and bet against any stock or industry that will suffer from higher interest rates. Here are two lists of strategies, some of which might be appropriate for you.

Consider these general ways to hedge real estate risk.

- Convert any adjustable rate mortgages to fixed rate mortgages.
- Move from a high-priced area to a low-priced area.
- Short ETFs that go down in value when interest rates rise.
- Short ETFs of the financial sector.
- Short real estate investment trusts (REITs).
- Short banking stocks.
- Short Fannie Mae and Freddie Mac.
- Short homebuilders.
- Short mortgage insurance companies.

Here are some specific investments to hedge real estate risk.

- You can make money when interest rates rise by shorting the iShares bond index (IEF).
- Financial stocks generally decline in price when interest rates rise. Short the entire financial sector by using the VFH, XLF, or IYF.
- REITs (real estate investment trusts) tend to do poorly in rising interest rate environments because their underlying real estate assets are highly leveraged and they are interest rate sensitive. Four ETFs representing the industry are the VNQ, ICF, RWR, and IYR. Direct plays on REITs include General Growth (GGP) and Rouse (RSE).
- Major commercial banks hold $1.5 trillion in outstanding mortgages. A rise in foreclosures, caused by higher interest rates, will dramatically affect their earnings. Consider shorting the Philadel-

phia Bank Index (BKX), JP Morgan Chase (JPM), Bank of America (BAC) and Citibank © (C).

- Together, Fannie Mae (FNM) and Freddie Mac (FRE) hold $3.7 trillion of residential mortgages. If foreclosures rise, both their income streams and profit margins will shrink, causing their stock prices to decline.

- If interest rates rise, fewer people will buy homes. Major homebuilders at risk include Hovnanian (HOV), Centex CTX), Beazer Homes (BZH), Ryland Group (RYL), and KB Home (KBH).

- If the housing market begins to slide, private mortgage insurers will sell less PMI and they will face defaults from current customers. Five companies most at risk include MGIC Corporation (MGIC), the PMI Group (PMI), the Radian Group (RDN), Old Republic Insurance (ORI), and Triad Guaranty Company (TGIC).

Before going further, I want to warn you that shorting stocks is very risky, and I recommend it only for experienced traders. Additionally, you should only consider using options if you are experienced in that area of trading. Finally, always seek the help of an experienced financial professional before implementing any ideas you get from this book.

No one can foretell the future with certainty. However, you have learned that real estate has historically been a good hedge against inflation. While market downturns are possible, it is likely that they will be short-lived. Therefore, you may want to consider any market weakness as an opportunity to accumulate property. Moreover, because you learned how to hedge your real estate risk, real estate investing should make even more sense to you. In real estate, everyone has a story. What story will you tell your children or grandchildren in twenty years?

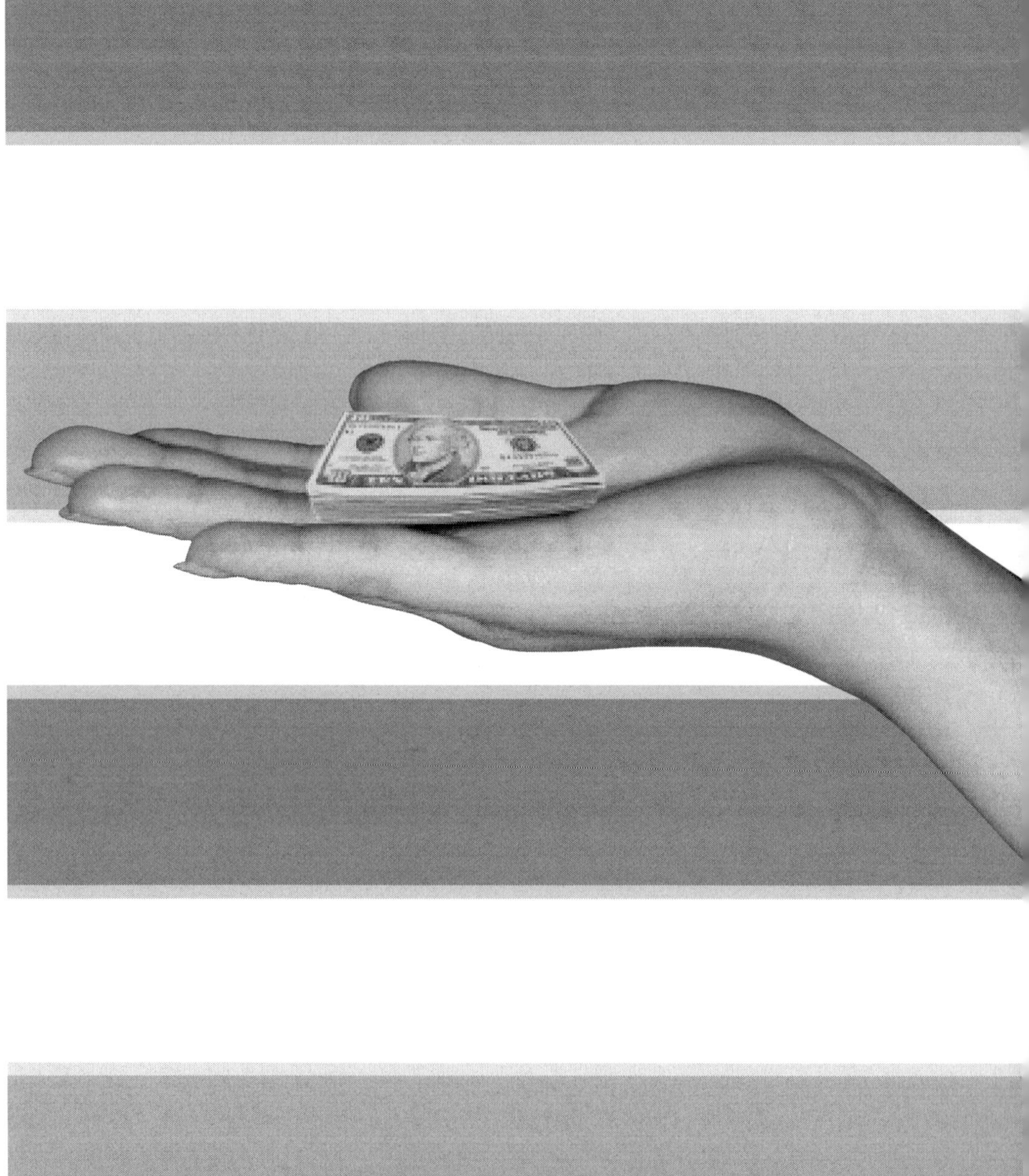

Epilogue

Picture yourself with a copy of the July 30, 2016 *New York Times* on your lap. Where is the Dow? What is the price of oil? Are there any natural disasters in the news? Are we at war? What is the price of gold? How much does an average house cost? What are the prevailing mortgage interest rates? The correct answers to those questions, if you could divine them, would certainly influence your investment strategy today.

In order to remain complacent and optimistic about the economy, the dollar, and the stock and bond markets, you would need to ignore completely all of the following facts.

- *Fact #1*
  Fiat money is a relatively new experiment in human history. To date, its failure rate has been 100 percent.

- *Fact #2*
  The amount of U.S. dollars now in the hands of China, Japan, and Saudi Arabia is staggering. So is the amount of U.S. debt. Should these countries decide to convert their dollars or invest elsewhere, the dollar will plummet and the cost of money will rise quickly.

- *Fact #3*

  The federal debt is exorbitant and getting worse every day. The interest on the debt will soon become a drag on the economy. Aside from raising taxes, the only way to reduce the federal debt is to promote inflation.

- *Fact #4*

  There is no money to pay for the baby boomers' Social Security retirement benefits. Either the government will need to raise taxes (impairing the economy), or it will need to borrow the money (forcing interest rates higher). The rapidly increasing costs of Medicare (the result of an aging population and higher medical costs) will have the same results.

- *Fact #5*

  The cost of healthcare (insurance and prescription drugs) is rising far faster than the CPI is.

- *Fact #6*

  We are rapidly running out of oil, and energy in the near future will be much more expensive than it is today. This will act to increase inflation and decrease corporate profits.

- *Fact #7*

  Global warming is reaching a tipping point, where climate induced damages could rise dramatically.

- *Fact #8*

  As China and other developing countries compete with the United States for scarce resources, they will bid up the price of those resources, adding further inflationary pressures.

- *Fact #9*

  The administration will need to continue to increase defense spending in order to achieve its intended foreign policy goals, and it will need to go deeper in debt to do that.

- *Fact #10*
  Members of the Federal Reserve, on more than one occasion, have stated that they intend to print money rather than risk deflation.

In the face of these facts, the risk of doing nothing or following the party line without thinking independently is great. You face risks on several fronts. First, you risk loss of purchasing power. That occurs when your money does not grow as fast as the price of items you want to buy.

Your second risk is currency risk. All your savings are denominated in dollars. When the value of the dollar falls, so does the value of your savings on the world market. Foreigners can outbid you for American goods, services, and even real estate by converting their more valuable currencies to dollars and then competing in our marketplace. They are able to buy more from America, but it will cost you more when you wish to purchase a BMW or take a European vacation. If the dollar falls in value, your money shrinks in the world marketplace.

Your third risk is market risk. As we have stated before, the data overwhelmingly shows that the stock market is likely to struggle for some time and could even fall dramatically. If you have invested the bulk of your savings in mutual funds, your savings are at great risk.

Your fourth risk is interest-rate risk. If you have an adjustable rate mortgage, you are at risk if short-term interest rates increase; if you own bonds, you are at risk if long-term interest rates increase.

You must determine the best way to reduce your purchasing power risk, currency risk, market risk, and interest-rate risk. You have three options to reduce your risks.

1. Get out of everything you own that will likely decline in value in an inflationary scenario and get into investments that you think will go up.
2. Keep what you have, but hedge to offset potential losses.
3. Take a portion of your equity and purchase assets that will likely

go up in value to offset a possible decline in value of other assets you hold.

You will hear many heated arguments over whether the country is headed for inflation or deflation. Consumer prices as measured by the CPI may remain relatively tame as the prices of common household items benefit from lower labor costs of Asian exporters. However, as the supplies of important natural resources diminish and growing world demand bids up the costs of inputs of production, even the price of certain consumer items could begin to rise. More importantly, we could experience inflation in some sectors and industries and deflation in others.

We are rapidly approaching an economic tipping point. The Federal Reserve has the power to tilt the scales toward either inflation or deflation. Because it has publicly stated its opposition to deflation, inflation is the more likely scenario. The next ten to fifteen years could resemble the 1970s — a period when stocks and bonds underperformed inflation, while commodities provided the best return for investors. Table E.1 shows the relative returns of asset classes during that period.

The Ball Is in Your Court

The foundation of long-term investment success lies in understanding the big picture and having an informed perspective. In this book, you learned how inflation has shaped world history and you became an expert on the seven major geopolitical trends that will promote the coming inflation and shape your financial destiny. You also learned what actions you must take to survive and profit. It is now time for you to take action.

Begin by assessing your current situation. Are you comfortable that your investments will outpace the coming inflation? If not, re-examine the three options I gave you in the last section and write down or circle the approach that most appeals to you. Then, look back through the book and pick one or two strategies to implement. Do not try to do too much at one time. It is better to start small and monitor the economy and selected markets rather than to plunge. Most importantly, remember to check the book's website (www.HoneyWhoShrunkOurMoney.com) for updates, my latest thoughts, and current recommendations. Until then,

Table E.1 Asset Prices Relative to Inflation, 1968 – 1979

Gold	19.4%
Silver	15.7%
Farmland	11.3%
Single-family homes	9.8%
INFLATION	6.5%
Bonds	5.8%
Stocks	3.1%

I hope the information I have provided has contributed to your understanding of the crises our country faces and our government's most likely responses, and I certainly hope you will *protect your savings and profit from America's woes.*

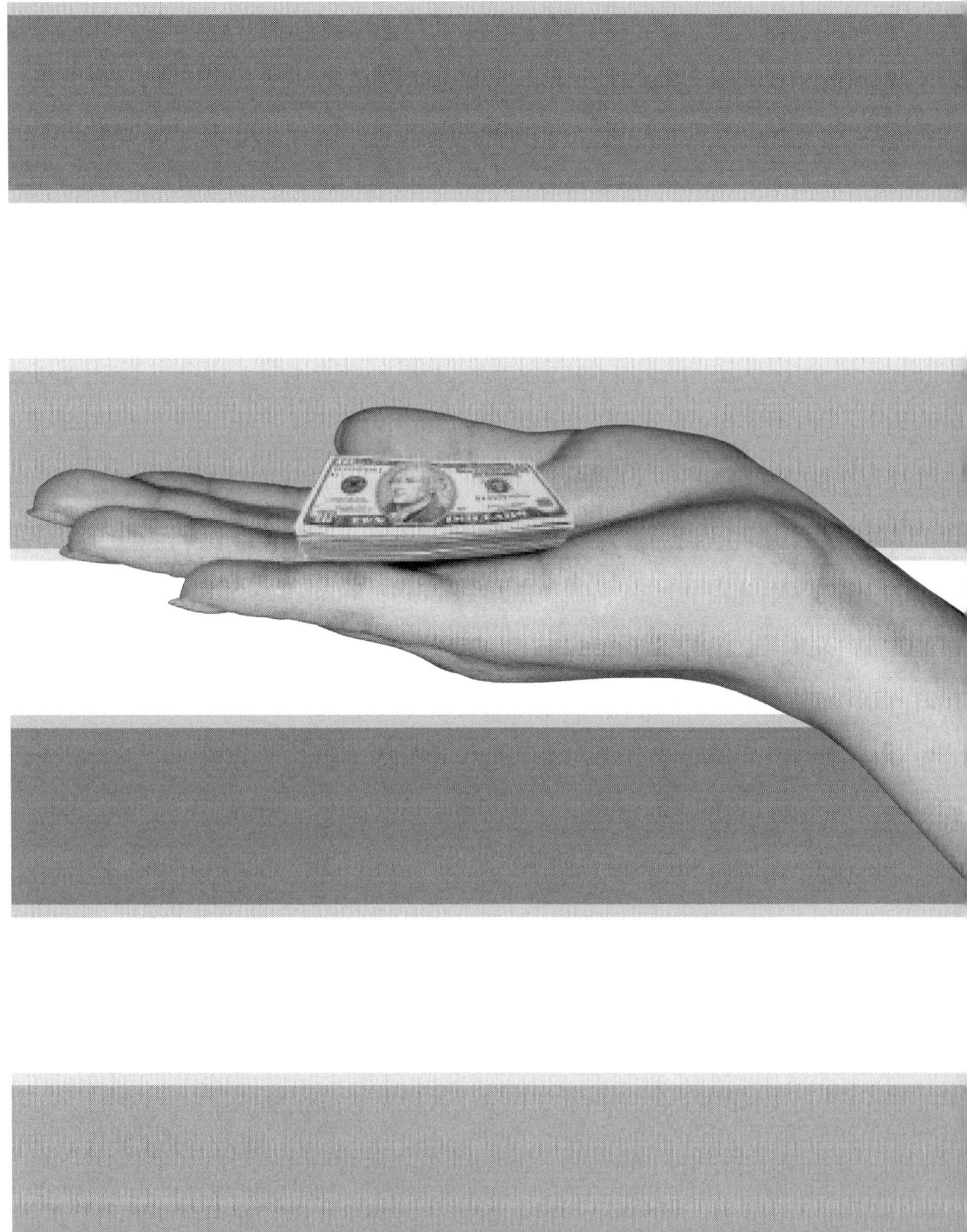

Final Word

Depending on when you read this book, some of the events I have predicted may have already occurred. Others may be just happening. Still others may seem quite remote. Markets may have already moved considerably in the direction I predicted or may indeed appear to be trending completely opposite to my predictions. In either case, don't discount what you have just learned. The historical precedents of thousands of years of civilization and the implications of fiat money and debt will not be changed by short-term interruptions of those trends.

Remember that the seven geopolitical crises I have detailed are not going to go away. They are like ticking times bombs. Don't be lulled into somnolence. Instead, take advantage of any respites to get your financial house in order. In the short term, the Federal Reserve has some control over markets, but that control is an art, not an exact science. More often then not, in their efforts to fine-tune the economy, they tend to overdo. If the Federal Reserve maintains a monetary policy that is too restrictive, the American economy will slip into a recession. If that were to happen, China's economy, which is highly dependent on the American consumer, would slow and demand for natural resources would weaken. That would cause sharp price setbacks in many of the commodities and natural resources recommended in this book.

Thus, as in all things in life: timing is everything. The Chinese economy is rapidly becoming self-sustaining and with each passing year it will become less dependent on the American consumer. Moreover, any recession in America will be short-lived because the Federal Reserve will quickly flood the system with monetary stimulus, which later will cause a further rise in asset prices. Thus, any setbacks in the market trends I have predicted should be welcomed as buying opportunities rather than myopically viewed as counter-evidence to those predictions.

Because timing is critical, I have created a website and a monthly e-zine, The Curtis Arnold Report, to keep you updated on the seven geopolitical crises (ticking time bombs) and my thoughts on current market conditions. As a reader of this book, you are entitled to receive this monthly report at no cost. Simply go to www.curtisarnold.com to sign up today.

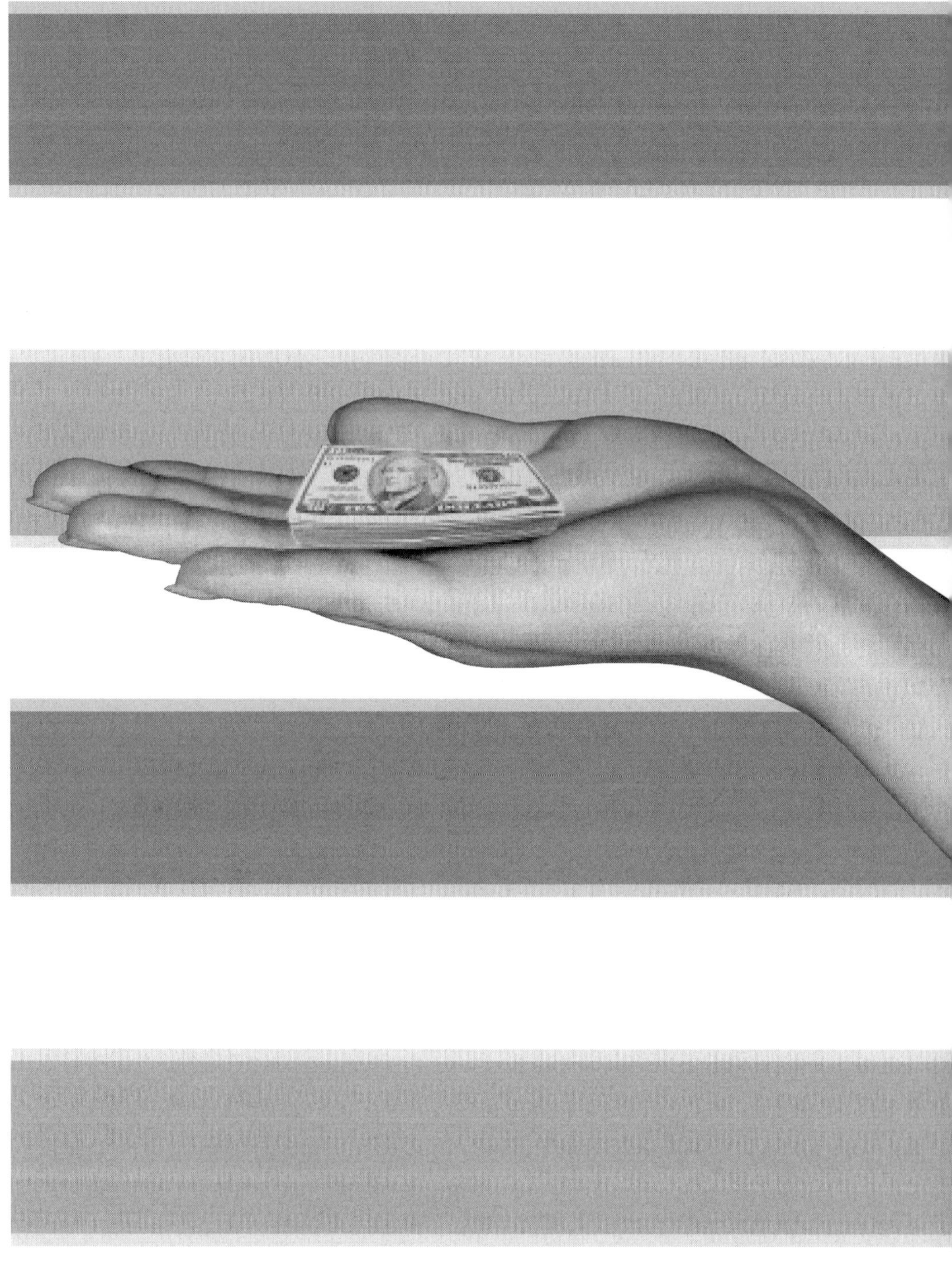

Endnotes

Part 1

1.   http://en.thinkexist.com/search/searchquotation.asp
?search=crises&q

Chapter 1

1. John Maynard Keynes, *Essays in Persuasion* (1931), chapter 2.
2. Andy Grove, keynote address to Business Software Alliance, Washington D.C., October 9, 2003.
3. Chris Gentle, "The Cusp of a Revolution: How Offshoring will Transform the Financial Services Industry," Deloitte Research, April 2003.
4. Investment Company Institute, Mututal Fund Fact Book.
5. Jeffrey Laderman, "Wall Street Spin Game," *Business Week*, October 5, 1998, 148.

6. "Talking Up the Market," *Financial Times*, July 19, 1999.

Chapter 2

1. Alan Ahearne et al., "Preventing deflation: lessons from Japan's experience in the 1990s," International Finance Discussion Papers 729, Board of Governors of the Federal Reserve System (U.S.), 2002.

2. John Mitchell et al., *The New Economy of Oil: Impacts on Business, Geopolitics, and Society* (London: Earthscan Publications, 2001), 136.

3. Jimmy Carter, State of the Union Address, January 23, 1980, as published in the *New York Times*, January 24, 1980.

4. Paul Roberts, *The End of Oil* (New York: Houghton Mifflin Company, 2004), 111.

5. Roger Burbach, "Bush Ideologues Trump Big Oil Interests in Iraq," Redress Information & Analysis, www.redress.btinternet.co.uk/rburbach21.htm (accessed September 30, 2003).

6. World Resources Institute, *World Resources 1998-1999* (Oxford: Oxford University Press), 141.

7. "China's Car Sales Hit One Million for First Time," Reuters News Service, December 16, 2002.

8. "China's Boom adds to Global Warming Problem," *New York Times*, October 22, 2003.

9. "Car Makers Prepare Profit Road," *South China Morning Post*, June 11, 2002.

10. Robert A. Manning, *The Asian Energy Factor* (New York: Palgrave, 2000).

11. "China Demand Looks Strong," *Aviation Week and Space Technology*, March 16, 1998, 13.

12. Robert A. Manning, *The Asian Energy Factor* (New York: Palgrave, 2000), 70.

13. Gale E. Christianson, *Greenhouse: The 200-Year Story of Global Warming* (New York: Penguin, 2000).

14. Thomas Karl et al., "Trends in U.S. Climate During the Twentieth Century," *Consequences*, Spring 1995.

15. Thomas, J. Crowley, "Causes of Climate Change over the Past 1000 Years," *Science*, July 14, 2000, 289.

16. Stephan Rahmstorf, "Risk of sea-change in the Atlantic," Potsdam Institute for Climate Impacts Research, *Nature*, August 28, 1997, 388.

17. Svein Sterhus, University of Bergen, *New Scientist*, November 27, 1999.

18. Robert Gagosian, Woods Hole Oceanographic Institution, see http://www.shoi.edu, 2002.

19. Ibid.

20. Walter C. Oechel, "Rachel's Environment and Health Weekly," #664, August 19, 1999.

21. "Climate Collapse: The Pentagon's Weather Nightmare," *Fortune*, January 26, 2004.

22. "160,000 Said Dying Yearly from Global Warming," Reuters News Service, October 1, 2003.

23. "Climate Change Will Harm Health," http://www.BBCNews.com, December 11, 2003.

24. "1998 a Disaster for Insurers, Leading Firm Says," Reuters News Service, January 18, 1999.

25. "Exxon Backs Groups That Question Global Warming," *New York Times*, May 28, 2003.

26. Senator James Inhofe, from a July 28, 2003 speech given on the Senate floor.

27. "U.S. Dashes Hopes for Climate Deal," *Guardian* (UK), May 14, 2002.

28. Guy Dauncey and Patrick Mazza, *Stormy Weather: 101 Solutions to Global Climate Change* (Canada: New Society Publishers, 2001), 5.

29. Peter G. Peterson, *Running on Empty* (New York: Farrar, Straus and Giroux, 2004).

30. www.whitehouse.gov/nsc/nss.html, release date September 17, 2002.

31. www.newamericancentury.org/RebuildingAmericasDefenses.pdf

32. Anna Dolgov, *Boston Globe*, February 21, 2004.

Part 2

1. http://en.thinkexist.com/search/searchquotation.asp
   ?search=crises&q

Chapter 3

1. Ralph Waldo Emerson, *The Conduct of Life*, 1860.

2. Peter Elkind, "Where Mary Meeker Went Wrong," *Fortune*,
   May 14, 2001, 78.

3. Edward Winslow, *Blind Faith* (San Francisco: Berrett-Koehler,
   2003), 79-80.

4. Alan Abelson, "Fun and Games," *Barron's*, November 12, 2001.

5. *Canadian Business*, April 16, 2001, 24.

6. Christopher Palmeri and Steven Brull, "If You've Got It, Spend
   It," *Business Week*, October 16, 2000.

7. Louis Lavelle, "Executive Pay," *Business Week*, April 16, 2001,
   79.

8. Geoffrey Colvin, "The Great CEO Pay Heist," *Fortune*, June 25,
   2001.

9. Ibid.

10. Institute for Policy Studies and United for a Fair Economy,
    "The 1990s: A Decade of Greed," Eighth Annual Report on
    Executive Excess, August 28, 2001.

11. Executive Pay Watch 2000, www.aflcio.org.

12. Edward Winslow, *Blind Faith* (San Francisco: Berrett-Koehler,
    2003), 96-97.

13. Burton G. Malkiel, *A Random Walk Down Wall Street* (New
    York: W.W. Norton, 1985).

14. Charles Ellis, *Winning the Losers Game* (New York: Mc-Graw-Hill,
    1998), 5.

15. Jonathan Clements, "Stock Funds Just Don't Measure Up," *Wall
    Street Journal*, October 5, 1999, C1.

16. Max Isaacman, *How to Be an Index Investor* (New York: Mc-Graw-Hill, 2000).
17. Edward Winslow, *Blind Faith* (San Francisco: Berrett-Koehler, 2003), 14.
18. "Quantitative Analysis of Investor Behavior," www.dalbarinc.com, June 21, 2001.
19. Jason Zweig, "What Fund Investors Really Need to Know," *Money*, June 2002, 110-115.
20. "Retirement out of Reach," Economic Policy Institute Briefing Paper, August 2002.

Chapter 4

1. http://www.quotationspage.com/quotes/John_Maynard_Keynes/

Chapter 5

1. http://www.quotationspage.com/quotes/Jackie_Mason

Chapter 6

1. http://www.brainyquote.com/quotes/quotes/j /jimrogers271613.html
2. Marc Levy, Associated Press, *Star Telegram*, January 8, 2005.

Chapter 7

1. http://www.quotationspage.com/quotes/Thomas_Jefferson/
2. The Independent, May 24, 2004.

Chapter 8

1. http://www.brainyquote.com/quotes/authors/a /alan_greenspan.html

Chapter 9

1. http://www.brainyquote.com/quotes/authors/m /marcus_tullius_cicero.html

Chapter 10

1. "Notes on the Next War: A Serious Topical Letter," *Esquire*, September 1935.
2. Jimmy Carter, State of the Union Address, January 23, 1980, as published in the *New York Times*, January 24, 1980.
3. "The Russian Federation Military Doctrine," *Arms Control Today*, May 2000, 29-38.
4. Ben Barber, "Beijing Eyes South China Sea with Sub Purchase," *Washington Times*, March 7, 1995.
5. "National Defense Program Outline in and After Fiscal Year 1996," Japanese Ministry of Foreign Affairs, August 7, 1997
6. www.newamericancentury.org/RebuildingAmericasDefenses.pdf.
7. "Making a Mint Inside the Iron Triangle of Defense, Government, and Industry," *Red Herring*, January 8, 2002.

Chapter 11

1. http://www.brainyquote.com/quotes/authors/d/donald_trump.html
2. Field Guide to Quick Real Estate Statistics, www.realtor.org/lib-web.nsf/pages/fg006
3. Elizabeth Warren and Amelia Warren Tyagi, *The Two Income Trap: Why Middle-Class Mothers and Fathers Are Going Broke* (New York: Basic Books, 2003).
4. "Eastward Ho!" *Palm Beach Post*, October 5, 2003.

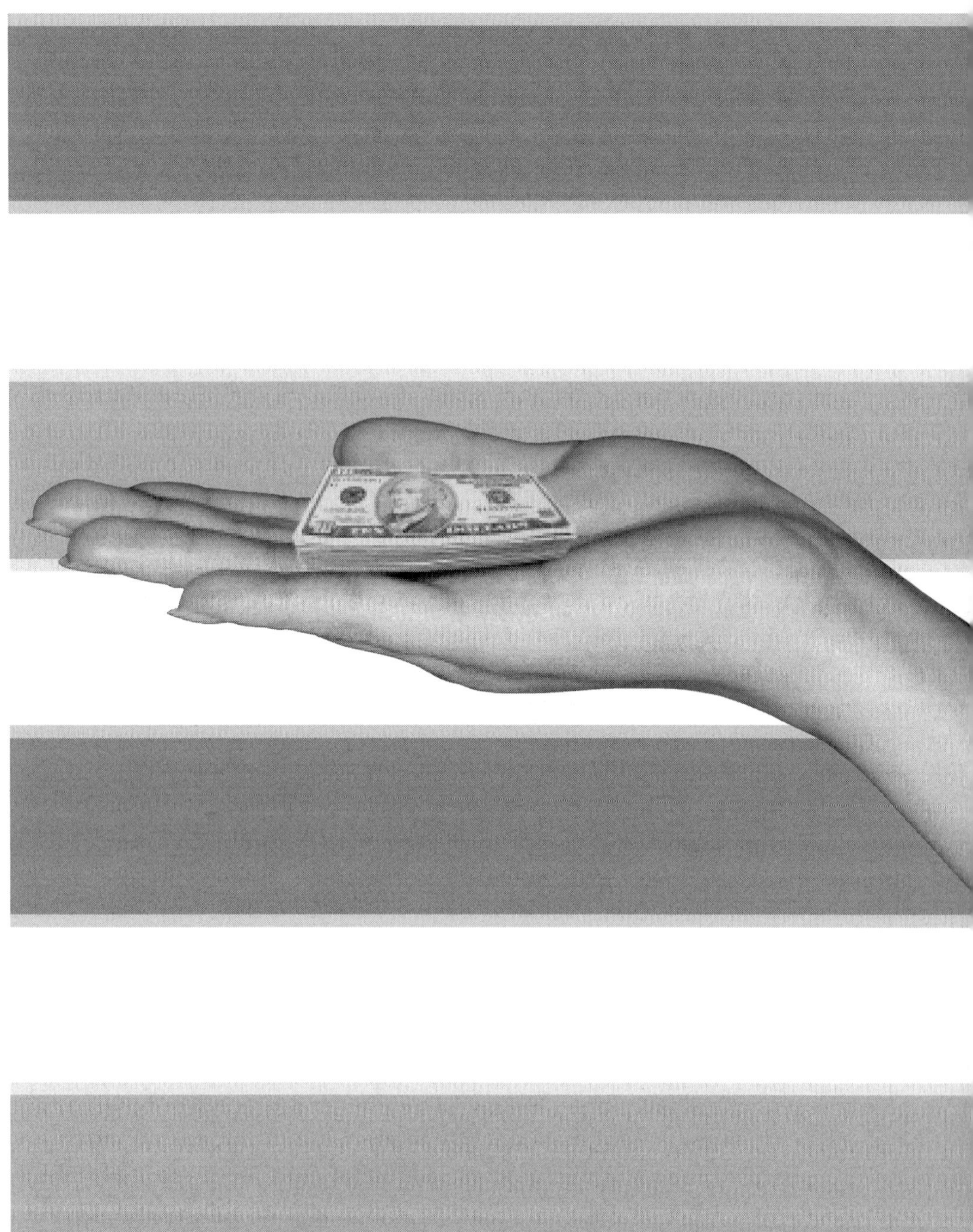

Bibliography

Angell, Marcia, M.D. *The Truth about Drug Companies*. New York: Random House, 2004.

Appleby, Julie. "Hospitals, Patients Run Short." *USA Today*, July 11, 2001.

Arms Control Today. "The Russian Federation Military Doctrinc." May 2000, 29-38.

Ball, Phil. "Reading the Signs." *Nature*, June 10, 1999.

Barber, Ben. "Beijing Eyes South China Sea with Sub Purchase." *Washington Times*, March 7, 1995.

Bartlett, Donald L. and James B. Steele. *Critical Condition*. New York: Doubleday, 2004.

Blank, Robert. *The Price of Life: The Future of American Health Care*. New York: Columbia University Press, 1997.

Bodil Als-Nielsen, et al. "Association of Funding and Conclusions in Randomized Drug Trials." *Journal of the American Medical Association*, August 20, 2003, 921.

Bowman, Karlyn, "A Reaffirmation of Self-Reliance? A New Ethic of Self-Sufficiency?" *The Public Perspective*, February-March 1996.

Brown, Lester R. *Vital Signs 2000*. New York: W.W. Norton and the Worldwatch Institute, 2000.

Burn, Timothy. "The Hunt for New Oil." *Washington Times*, September 28, 2003.

Campbell, Colin. *The Coming Oil Crisis*. Essex, England: Multi-Science Publishing Company and Petroconsultants, 1998.

Christianson, Gale E. *The 200-Year Story of Global Warming*. Berkley: Greystone, 1999.

Clements, Jonathan. "Stock Funds Just Don't Measure Up," *Wall Street Journal*, October 5, 1999, C1.

Clements, Jonathan, "Not Everyone Can Pick Funds, Really," *Wall Street Journal*, November 9, 1999, Sec. C.

Colvin, Geoffrey. "The Great CEO Pay Heist." *Fortune*, June 25, 2001.

Crowley, Thomas, J. "Causes of Climate Change over the Past 1000 Years." *Science*, July 14, 2000.

Dauncey, Guy and Patrick Mazza. *Stormy Weather: 101 Solutions to Global Climate Change*. Canada: New Society Publishers, 2001.

Davies, Glyn. *A History of Money From Ancient Times to the Present Day*. Cardiff, Wales: University of Wales Press, 2002.

Dent, J.M., ed. *The Travels of Marco Polo*. London, 1908.

Dunn, Seth and Christopher Flavin. "Destructive storms drive insurance losses up: will taxpayers have to bail out insurance industry?" Washington, DC: Worldwatch Institute, 1999.

Economic Policy Institute. "Retirement Out of Reach." Economic Policy Institute Briefing Paper, August 2002.

Elkind, Peter. "Where Mary Meeker Went Wrong." *Fortune*, May 14, 2001.

Ellis, Charles. *Winning the Losers Game*. New York: Mc-Graw-Hill, 1998.

European Wind Energy Association. "Record Growth for Global Wind." Press release, March 3, 2003.

Easterling, David, et al. "Temperature Range Narrows Between Daytime Highs and Nighttime Lows." *Science*, July 18, 1997.

Famighetti, Robert, ed. *World Almanac and Book of Facts 2000*. New York: St. Martin's, 2000.

FDA website: www.fda.gov/cder/rdmt/pstable.htm.

Feldman, Amy. "Sue Your Broker." *Money*, October 2001.

Field Guide to Quick Real Estate Statistics, www.realtor.org/libweb.nsf/pages/fg006

Fischer, Irving. *The Purchasing Power of Money*. New York: Macmillan, 1929.

Friedman, Milton. *Money Mischief*. New York: Harcourt Brace and Company, 1994.

Fortune. "Climate Collapse: the Pentagons Weather Nightmare." January 26, 2004.

Friends of the Earth. *Friends of the Earth 2000*. "Paying for Pollution." http://www.foe.org/camps/eco/payingforpollution/intro.html.

Fuchs, Victor. "What Every Philosopher Should Know About Health Economics." *Health Economics*, June 1996.

Gagosian, Robert, Woods Hole Oceanographic Institution. http://www.shoi.edu, 2002.

Galbraith, J. K. *The Great Crash of 1929*. New York: Mariner Books, 1997.

Gelbspan, Ross. *Boiling Point*. New York: Basic Books, 2004.

————. *The Heat Is On*. New York: Basic Books, 1998.

Geller, Howard. *Energy Revolution: Policies for a Sustainable Future*. Washington D.C.: Island Press, 2003.

Gentle, Chris. "The Cusp of a Revolution: How Offshoring will Transform the Financial Services Industry." Deloitte Research, April 2003.

Glick, Daniel. "Global Warming: Bulletins from a Warmer World." *National Geographic*, September 2004.

Goodrich, L.C. *A Short History of the Chinese People*. Mineola, NY: Dover Publications, 2002.

Gosh, Chandrani and Andrew Tanzer. "Patent Play." *Forbes*, September 17, 2001, 141.

Graig, Laurene. *Health of Nations: An International Perspective on U.S. Health Care Reform*. Washington, DC: CQ Press, 1999.

Grove, Andy. Keynote address to Business Software Alliance, Washington DC, October 9, 2003.

Hadley Centre for Climate Research, "Forest and soils may speed up global warming," UK, Nov 8, 1998.

Hakim, Danny. "Cloaked in Green, but Guzzling Gas." *New York Times*, April 19, 2003.

Hamilton, Earl J. *American Treasure and the Price Revolution in Spain, 1501-1650*. Cambridge, MA: Harvard University Press, 1934.

Howard, Philip K. "Legal Malpractice." *Wall Street Journal*, January 27, 2003.

Huntington, Samuel P. *The Clash of Civilizations and the Remaking of World Order*. New York: Touchstone Books, 1997.

Inhofe, Senator James. From a speech given on the Senate floor, July 28, 2003.

Institute for Policy Studies and United for a Fair Economy. "The 1990s: A Decade of Greed." Eighth Annual Report on Executive Excess. August 28, 2001.

Investment Company Institute. *Mutual Fund Fact Book*. Washington DC: Investment Company Institute, 1999.

IPCC Report. *Climate Change 2001: The Scientific Basis*. Intergovernmental Panel on Climate Change, 2001.

Isaacman, Max. *How to Be an Index Investor*. New York: McGraw-Hill, 2000.

Johnston, David, et al. "Al-Qaeda's New Links Increase Threats From Far-Flung Sites." *New York Times*, June 16, 2002

Jones, Jeffrey. *The State and Emergence of the British Oil Industry*. London: MacMillan, 1981.

Kahil, Raouf. *Inflation and Economic Development in Brazil, 1946-1963*. Oxford: Clarendon Press, 1973.

Karl, Thomas, et al. "Trends in U.S. Climate During the Twentieth Century." *Consequences*, Spring 1995.

Kessler, Daniel P. "Is Hospital Competition Socially Wasteful?" *The Quarterly Journal of Economics* 115 (2000).

Kohn, Linda T., et al. "To Err is Human." Washington DC: Institute of Medicine, 2000.

Kondro, Wayne and Barbara Sibbald. "Drug Company Experts Advised Staff to Withhold Data About SSRI Use in Children." *Canadian Medical Association Journal*, March 2, 2004.

Krugman, Paul. *The Great Unraveling: Losing Our Way in the New Century*. New York: W.W. Norton & Company, 2004.

Laderman, Jeffrey. "Wall Street Spin Game." *Business Week*, October 5, 1998.

Lamm, Richard, D. *The Brave New World of Health Care*. Colorado: Fulcrum Publishing, 2003.

Lave, Charles. "A New CAFÉ." *Access Magazine* (University of California, Berkeley, Transportation Center), Fall 2001.

Lavelle, Louis. "Executive Pay." *Business Week*, April 16, 2001.

Leeb, Stephen. *The Oil Factor*. New York: Warner Books, 2004.

Leggett, Jeremy. *Carbon War: Global Warming and the End of the Oil Era*. New York: Routledge, 2001

Lockwood, M., et al. "A Doubling of the Sun's Coronal Magnetic Field during the Past 100 Years." *Nature*, 399 (1999): 437.

Los Angeles Times. "Subverting U.S. Health." Editorial. December 7, 2003, sec. A1.

Lueck, Sarah. "Drug Prices Far Outpace Inflation." *Wall Street Journal*, July 10, 2003.

Malkiel, Burton G. *A Random Walk Down Wall Street*. New York: W.W. Norton, 1985.

Managed Care Weekly Digest. "Businesses anticipate increases in healthcare insurance costs." *Managed Care Weekly Digest*, April 7, 2003.

Manning, Robert A. *The Asian Energy Factor*. New York: Palgrave, 2000.

Martens, Willem J. M., et al. "Potential Impact on Global Climate Change on Malaria Risk." *Environmental Health Perspectives*, May 1995.

McLean, Bethany. "Hear No Risk, See No Risk, Speak No Risk." *Fortune*, May 14, 2001.

Mitchell, John, et al. *The New Economy of Oil: Impacts on Business, Geopolitics, and Society*. London: Earthscan Publications, 2001.

Obaid, Nawaf E., et al. "The Sino-Saudi Energy Rapproachement: Implications for u.s. National Security." Report prepared for the Office of the Secretary of Defense, u.s. Department of Defense, January 8, 2002.

Oechel, Walter C. "Rachel's Environment and Health Weekly" #664, August 19, 1999.

Okie, Susan. "Missing Data on Celebrex: Full Study Altered Picture of Drug." Washington Post, August 5, 2001, Sec A.

O'Ryan, Raul, D. *Transportation in Developing Countries: Greenhouse Gas Scenario for Chile*. Arlington, VA: Pew Center on Global Climate Change, August 2002.

Paarlberg, Don. *An Analysis and History of Inflation*. Westport, CT: Praeger Publishers, 1993.

Palmeri, Christopher and Steven Brull. "If You've Got It, Spend It." *Business Week*, October 16, 2000.

Pear, Robert. "Drug Companies Increase Spending on Efforts to Lobby Congress and Governments." *New York Times*, September 5, 2003.

———. "Democrats Demand Inquiry into Charge by Medicare Officer." *New York Times*, March 14, 2004

Petersen, Melody. "Drug Shortages Become a Worry at Hospitals around the Country." *New York Times*, January 3, 2001.

Physicians Desk Reference. 56th ed. Montvale, NJ: Thompson PDR, 2002.

Prechter, Robert. R., Jr. *Conquer the Crash*. New Jersey: John Wiley & Sons, 2002.

Rahmstorf, Stephan. "Risk of Sea-Change in the Atlantic." *Nature*, August 28, 1997.

Reuters News Service. "China Car Sales Hit One Million for First Time." December 16, 2002.

Reuters News Service. "160,000 Said Dying Yearly from Global Warming." October 1, 2003.

Reuters News Service. "1998 a Disaster for Insurers, Leading Firm Says." January 18, 1999.

Reuters New Service. "State Officials Want Bush to Act on Global Warming." July 18, 2002.

Reuters News Service. "EU Says Climate Strategy Integral to U.S. Relations." March 23, 2001.

Revkin, A. and K. Seelye. "Report by the E.P.A. Leaves Out Data on Climate Change." *New York Times*, June 19, 2003.

Riva, Joseph P., Jr. "World Oil Production After the Year 2000: Business as Usual or Crises?" www.ncseonline.org.

Roberts, Paul. *The End of Oil*. New York: Houghton Mifflin Company, 2004.

Rogers, Jim. *Hot Commodities*. New York: Random House, 2004.

Sachs, Jeffrey. "Social Conflict and Populist Policies in Latin America." National Bureau of Economic Research, Working Paper 2897 (March 1989).

Schurr, Sam H., et al. *Energy in the American Economy, 1850-1975: An Economic Study of Its History and Prospects*. Baltimore: Johns Hopkins University Press, 1960.

Shiller, Robert, J. *Irrational Exuberance*. New York: Broadway Books, 2000.

Smil, Vaclav. *Energy in World History*. Boulder: Westview Press, 1994.

———. *Energy at the Crossroads: Global Perspectives and Uncertainties*. Cambridge, MA: MIT Press, 2003.

Stelfox, H. T., et al. "Conflict of Interest in the Debate over Calcium Channel Antagonists." New England Journal of Medicine, January 8, 1998, 101.

Stolberg, Sheryl Gay and Gardiner Harris. "Industry Fights to Put Imprint on Drug Bill." *New York Times*, September 5, 2003

Talbott, John, R. *The Coming Crash in the Housing Market*. New York: McGraw Hill, 2003.

Te Brake, William H. "Air Pollution and Fuel Crises in Preindustrial London, 1250-1650." In Technology and the West: A Historical Anthology from Technology and Culture, ed. Terry S. Reynolds and Stephen H. Cutcliffe. Chicago: University of Chicago Press, 1997.

Thompson, David, J. "The Seasons, Global Temperature, and Precession." *Science*, April 7, 1995.

Topfer, Klaus. United Nations Environment Program, commenting on the IPCC's Third Assessment Report, January 2001.

Trenberth, Kevin E. The Extreme Weather Events of 1997 and 1998." *Consequences*, 1999.

USA Today. "Drugmakers' gifts to Doctors Finally Get Needed Scrutiny." Editorial. October 14, 2002, Sec. A.

U.S. Congress, Joint Economic Committee. "The Benefits of Medical Research and the Role of the NIH." Washington, DC, May 2000.

U.S. Department of Energy, Energy Information Administration. *International Energy Outlook 1999.*Washington DC.

U.S. Department of Energy, Energy Information Administration. *International Energy Outlook 2000*. Washington DC.

U.S. Department of Health and Human Services. *For a Healthy Nation 2000*. Washington, DC.

U.S. National Intelligence Council. *Global Trends 2010*. Washington DC, 1997.

U.S. Securities and Exchange Commission. "Special Study: On-Line Brokerage: Keeping Apace of Cyberspace." Washington, DC, 1999.

Warren, Elizabeth and Amelia Warren Tyagi. *The Two Income Trap: Why Middle-Class Mothers and Fathers Are Going Broke*. New York: Basic Books, 2003.

Weisbrot, Mark. "Why Housing Is about to Go Pop." *Business Week*, April 12, 2004.

Williams, David. "Stealth Merger: Drug Companies and Government Medical Research." *Los Angeles Times*, December 7, 2003, sec. M.

Winslow, Edward. *Blind Faith*. San Francisco: Berrett-Koehler, 2003.

World Resources Institute. *World Resources 1998-1999*. Oxford: Oxford University Press.

Yergin, Daniel. *The Prize: The Epic Quest for Oil, Money & Power*. New York: Free Press, 1993.

Zweig, Jason. "What Fund Investors Really Need to Know." *Money*, June 2002.

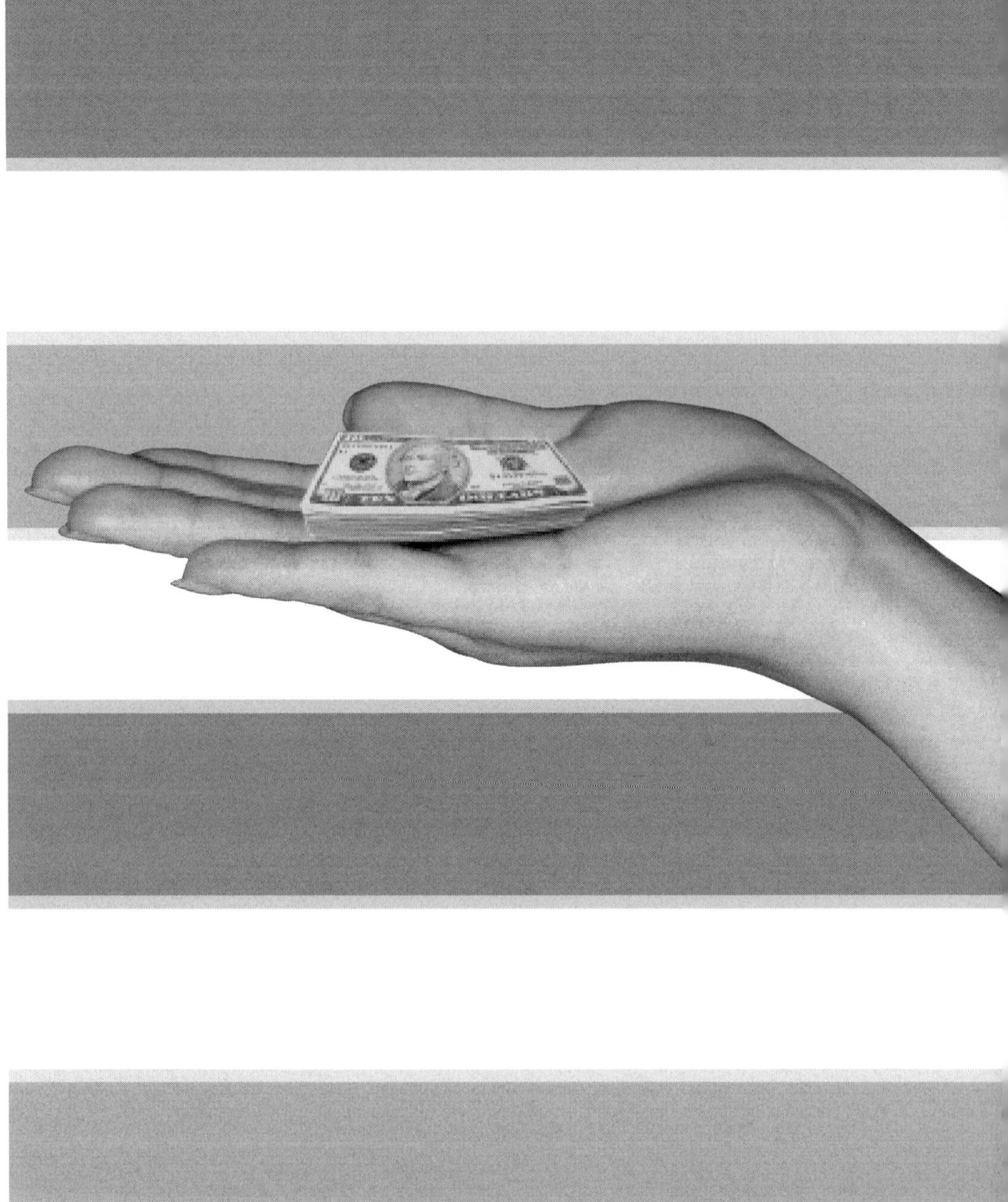

Index

Note: Information presented in tables and figures is denoted by *t* and *f* respectively.